Business insiders offer extraordinary praise for David Roper's
GETTING THE JOB YOU WANT...NOW!

"[A] bible on job seeking...David Roper is an absolute expert at what he does, and his new book is an extremely well-crafted written reflection of the techniques which have made him so well known in our area."
—Mort Ettinger, Chairperson, Department of Marketing, Salem State College, VP, Collegiate Liaison, AMA Member, AMA Senior Executive, Inner Circle

"Fascinating...Mr. Roper clearly understands where the jobs can be found and how important the résumé and follow-up is to success....Easy to read and right on target, the timing for this book is *now*!"
—Ron Hoffman, Executive Vice President, Human Resources, ALCOA

"Addresses the many challenges of competing in the tough job market in a comprehensive yet extremely readable manner. His experience, humor, and practical strategies are crucial tools for anyone engaged in a job search."
—Brian J. Smith, Director, Global Human Resources Strategy, Colgate-Palmolive Company

"Provides good and sound information."
—John J. Tucker, Senior Vice President, Human Resources, Philip Morris Companies, Inc.

"A bottom-line guide with innovative techniques for today's job hunter...excellent examples that are tied in well to job search techniques."
—R. Carter McLaughlin, Human Resources Staffing, BellSouth Corporation

"David Roper's book has it right! Follow his golden path, and it's hard to imagine a misstep on the job search road."
—Joyce Bartlett, President, Bartlett & Wickham Associates, Inc.

GETTING THE JOB YOU WANT ...NOW!

DAVID H. ROPER

50 Winning Moves for Spotting Hot Companies, Identifying Hiring Patterns, and Landing a Great Job

WARNER BOOKS

A Time Warner Company

To M.K., Nicholas, and Allison

Warner Books, Inc., 1271 Avenue of the Americas, New York, NY 10020

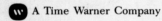 A Time Warner Company

Printed in the United States of America

First Warner Books Printing: February 1994

10 9 8 7 6 5 4 3 2 1

Library of Congress Cataloging-in-Publication Data
Roper, David H.
    Getting the job you want—now! / David H. Roper.
      p.   cm.
    ISBN 0-446-39451-3
    1. Job hunting—United States.   2. Résumés (Employment)
I. Title.
HF5382.75.U6R67   1994
650.14—dc20   93-3339
                                                 CIP

Cover design: Don Puckey
Book design: H. Roberts

Contents

II. MARKETING YOURSELF

Winning Moves

III. SELLING YOURSELF

Winning Moves

IV. SHINING EXAMPLES:
Winning Moves from Street-Savvy Job Seekers

Winning Moves

Acknowledgments

My sincere thanks to my family, who never questioned, only supported, the long hours it took to complete this book.

To my wife, whose thought process so naturally complements my own, and whose editorial skills and support have made her the kind of mate/editor/friend that all authors dream about.

To Mauro DiPreta, my superb editor and friend at Warner Books.

To Shana Burg, who helped enormously with the development of this book.

To my agent, David Black, and his staff, who kept everything moving.

And to countless clients, whose personal job-search experiences gave me the knowledge and impetus to write this book for future job seekers.

Introduction

The country in which you and I live sheds thousands of jobs every month. By most estimates, there will be *more than 7 million active job seekers* in the United States by the mid-1990s. Virtually all observers of the U.S. labor market, from both sides of the political spectrum, agree that our job market has changed dramatically and will never again resemble that of the past three decades. Because of a highly layered work force (too many layers of management), fierce global competition, and a large national debt, we have entered an era of massive downsizing. Mobility is replacing security; job hopping—rather than long-term employee loyalty—is becoming the only way for most U.S. workers to get ahead, or, for that matter, even survive. Because of a new world of job instability and a highly competitive job market, for the first time in several decades, *nearly every employed worker has the mind-set of the heretofore-unemployed job seeker. As a result of this, a science of job seeking has become a necessity for both the employed and unemployed at all levels*. Yet this new science of job seeking exists in a world of relatively uneducated laymen.

No longer can the job seeker work in a reactive mode, waiting for opportunities. He must now become a HUNTER, making or uncovering opportunities. This book was written to help the job hunter do that by giving him a series of cutting-edge job-search tools—the Winning Moves of this book.

Over the past decade, the dramatic growth of A-Script, my own job-search consulting firm, has occurred primarily because of the effectiveness of the job-hunting tools and approaches I've given my clients. Many of these tools and techniques came to me through the actual experiences of my streetwise clients. Any intriguing job-search moves went into my "Winning Move" file. For 10 years I saved Winning Moves. Hundreds of them. What you are about to read are the real keepers. These Winning Moves work. The walls of my office waiting room are literally covered with thank-you letters from successful job-hunting clients.

Two years ago I knew it was time to compile these Winning Moves into one easy-to-follow format that would give today's job seekers a jump start.

This book is geared to the mind-set of the job seeker in a challenging job market. It is geared to the job seeker of this new decade of massive corporate downsizing. It is geared to the job seeker who wants something that goes down easily and works quickly. It is designed for the individuals who, like the end users of personal computers, don't want to know why it works, but simply *how to make it work*.

What follows, in 50 short, powerful chapters, will guide you through every stage of the job search—the motivating, marketing, and selling stages necessary for successful job hunting.

The Winning Moves you are about to read will give you the ability to:

- **Uncover** hidden market opportunities while other job seekers are headed toward the obvious, glutted markets.
- **Determine** your odds in your job-market assault, and compute how long it will take before you hit pay dirt.
- **Network** in a way that gets others to market you while you're marketing yourself.
- **Build** a powerful résumé that gives you immediate credibility.
- **Write** a job-search broadcast letter that hooks the reader and gets the prospective employer to call you!

- **Control** the interview in a manner that gets the interviewer to actually divulge what he wants in the ideal candidate.
- **Handle**—and even benefit from—rejection.
- **Manage** your time in a way that is both productive and positive to your self-esteem.

These and many other Winning Moves are waiting.
So is the job market.
Dig in!

I

Motivating Yourself

Winning Move #1:

Set a Goal—Because If You Don't Know Where You Want to Go, It Doesn't Matter Where You're Going

One Day Alice came to a fork in the road and saw a Cheshire cat in a tree. "Which road do I take?" she asked.

His response was a question: "Where do you want to go?"

"I don't know," Alice answered.

"Then," said the cat, "it doesn't matter."

—*Lewis Carroll*

Don't move your body yet. Don't call all your contacts. Don't borrow money. Don't spend money on job-search programs. Don't panic. Just stop.

You need a goal. You need a target. You need to ask some questions of yourself.

Jobs are nothing more than problems being solved. Jobs are formed because of good problems and because of bad problems. For example, a good problem is when a company gets a big new account. The solution to the problem could be increased account-management jobs. On the other hand, the mountain of toxic waste produced and stockpiled today is an example of a bad problem. One solution is the creation of new companies, and hence new jobs, to carry out proper disposal of hazardous waste.

Find a Problem That Concerns You— You'll Find a Job Right Behind It

Make a list of problems that concern you. These problems can be local, regional, national, or global. Put some thought into this. List as many of your interests and concerns about the world around you as you can. By doing so you have already narrowed down areas that you know will be fulfilling. Now, can any of your skills, aptitudes, or abilities contribute to the solutions of these problems? If the answer is yes, you now have a job target! Perhaps you'll need specialized schooling. Or perhaps you'll have to start at the bottom and work your way into the field. But at least you'll have some goals. And goals motivate. Motivation gives momentum. And momentum will bring you forward into an array of foreseeable and unforeseeable opportunities. Begin!

Winning Move #2:

Don't Depend on the Rabbit's Foot in the Job Search Game— Remember, It Didn't Work for the Rabbit

Why do I call something as serious as a job search a game? Because it has rules, and it requires concentration, forethought, strategies, dedication, and drive. And because you can win or lose, depending on how you play. There are good jobs and bad jobs everywhere. If you play the game well, chances are you will get one of the good ones. If you don't play well—if you rely on luck— chances are you will get one of the not-so-good ones.

In a job search you are facing one of the great challenges of your life. The choice of approach and attitude is all yours. You can look at this as either a game—a challenge to conquer—or as a long, laborious, stressful, and depressing experience. You can look at it as an opportunity to travel a path of great resistance, confusion, and uncertainty, and succeed. Or you can look at the job search as one with bad odds, depressing circumstances, and not much future.

Take your choice. It's all yours. If you've bought this book you're already ahead of your fellow job seekers. If you follow the moves, you'll win the game.

Win Yourself Over by Knowing the Odds Are with You

Getting the job you want is indeed very possible and probable. You will win because, believe it or not, *the odds are with you*. When you understand and believe this, your attitude will be one of anticipated success, not failure. You'll believe in yourself, not the other person. To prospective employers, you'll radiate confidence, not uncertainty or pessimism. People will want to get you, not want to get rid of you.

The Odds Are *with Me*, You Say?

Yes. For three reasons:

The Odds Are That the Job Market Will Be Getting Bigger.

Here is today's situation:

- The employment rate is 92 percent. Only 8 percent of us are unemployed. That means *your odds are 92 out of 100*. Where else do you get those kinds of odds?

- America is bursting with smaller, growing companies with job opportunities. In fact, **in 1993, the vast majority of the hiring in America was done by companies with fewer than 20 employees!** Don't think of big companies as your best or only source of jobs. We've all heard of the Fortune 500 corporations, yet what most job seekers don't realize is that there are *more than 15 million other companies in America!*
- There are *3 million new jobs* added to the U.S. labor force every year, and the labor force is shrinking! America is graying.
- People are staying healthy and living longer, causing more need for products and services, and hence more jobs. Right now there are 60 million Americans over the age of 50, and they control more than half of our country's assets and discretionary income. This population, soon to be combined with a large, retiring baby-boomer group, will dramatically increase the need for products and services (read: jobs) over the next 20 years. And who will supply that need? Who will fill those jobs? Only a meager work force resulting from the baby *bust* of the late 60s and 70s. Again, good odds!

The Odds Are That You Have Value

We all do. A heart surgeon has value and gets fulfillment by fixing people's hearts to prolong life. A school crossing guard has value keeping precious children safe from accidents, allowing them a prolonged life. Our value comes from our ability to contribute, at the level that's best matched with our knowledge, skills, aptitudes, and interests. So we all have value. And society has need. Increasing need.

The Odds Are That You Are Marketable

If you have value and there is a market, then you are marketable. It's just as simple as that.

Winning Move #4:

Understand That Most of Your "Competition" Is Totally Out to Lunch—It's You You've Got to Beat

We has met the enemy, and it is us!

—*Pogo*

Will your job search be successful? Once you've won yourself over, all that's left is the competition. Let's look them over:

Your competition is largely untrained, unskilled, uneducated, and poorly equipped for job seeking. Your competition takes many wrong turns, wastes time, broods, wallows in self-pity, and lowers their sights. Your competition waits for opportunities, rather than making them happen. Like lemmings, they wait or just follow, accepting what's doled out to them—blindly heading toward the cliffs and the crash.

Why, they're hardly competitors at all!

So let's forget about them, and concentrate on ourselves.

Winning Move #5:

Win the Job You Want by Becoming an Actor, a Sleuth, and a Salesman

Winning means becoming a versatile player. To win the right job, at times you'll need to play the roles of actor, sleuth, and salesman. You will need to act confident when you're not, uncover information about people and companies, and sell a very important product—yourself.

If you feel you're not innately one of these characters, don't worry. I'm not asking you to be a good actor, just to act. I'm not asking you to be Sherlock Holmes, just a basic investigator. I'm not asking you to be Zig Ziglar, just to apply some of the basic tenets of sales to sell something you know better than anyone else—yourself.

So, in this time of job seeking you'll be changing roles in time of need, like Clark Kent in the phone booth. By playing these roles with commitment, you'll have made a job-winning move.

Success in any job search requires motivational, marketing, and sales skills. Designed with that in mind, this book is broken up into sections titled Motivating Yourself, Marketing Yourself, and Selling Yourself. You're five chapters into the motivating section, so you've already moved forward in your job search. You know you have to set goals. You know you can't rely on luck alone. You know the odds are with you. And you know most of your competitors are out to lunch. And now you know you're going to stay motivated and confident. It's one of your roles.

Now let's keep moving.

Winning Move #6:

Start Looking for Your Next Job the Day You Get Your Present One

There is no job security anymore. Jobs and careers change faster now than ever before. Mergers and acquisitions, changing technologies, and global competition can cause an industry, a company, and its employees to become dinosaurs overnight. We are long past the era when loyalty and good performance ensured job security. This is not to suggest disloyalty to your employer, only to stress that loyalty alone is no longer enough to guarantee your job.

So where does job security come from?

Job security comes from taking responsibility for keeping your career as flexible as the times, as attuned to economic and demographic changes as possible. It is up to you to maintain your value in the job market. In the 1950s, 1960s, and even 1970s, an employer took care of this for you, telling you that you needed specialized training in this new area or in that different function. But in this new era of major company downsizing and restructuring, you're often told that your job is eliminated, not that you'll be retrained. So you need to develop contingency plans continually, because your first loyalty has to be to yourself. You cannot ensure your employment with your current employer. There are simply too many factors that are out of your control.

You must be ready to move *before* your company moves you out. You must maintain value in the marketplace, not just in your company. Your knowledge of where both your company *and* your industry are headed must always remain on the cutting edge.

Don't Be a Rising Star in a Falling Industry— Your Lights Will Go Out

Follow your industry very closely. Read good trend books and trade magazines for your industry, ones that base their judgments on statistics, demographics, technological changes, and economic needs. How do you find these? A good place to start is your industry association. Every industry of significant size has one or several professional associations serving it. These associations often make it their business to communicate their understanding of where their industry is going.

Go to your town or city library and consult the *Encyclopedia of Associations* and the *Directory of Directories*. These publications will take you to your industry associations. Call them. Get their literature. Maybe even join them. Find out which ones keep a pulse on your industry's future. From these associations you'll likely learn of specialized sub-industry publications and associations. You'll learn ahead of time what retraining or specialized experience will be valued in the future. You'll learn which companies, products, or services are likely to be outmoded or in vogue. Then you'll be able to act, rather than react. You'll know ahead of time if your industry value is intact or becoming outmoded.

Keep a proactive, rather than reactive, career management attitude. Be like the surfer. Endeavor to ride the crest of your industry. It's nice up there, up where the view is best and the opportunities are freshest—a place away from the trough. Don't let your career get lost in a world with little horizon, or you could get buried by the next wave of layoffs!

Winning Move #7:
Sell Yourself at Your Level of Competence, Not Below It and Not Above It

Appearing or being told you are overqualified is one of the more frustrating parts of job seeking. Why won't employers believe you when you insist you will be comfortable and productive at the level to which you are applying? Because the employer often has good reason for his feelings. Put yourself in his place. It costs him x number of dollars to advertise for someone. It costs him x number of dollars to train someone. He wants that someone to stay. If prospective employee "A" has a background that shows experience or training above and beyond the level of the available position, the employer is going to assume one of the following:

- "A" is either a person who has had personal problems or on-the-job difficulties (something the employer doesn't want to deal with) and therefore can't get back into the job market at his old level.
- "A" is, for whatever other reason, shooting too low and will soon outgrow the challenge of the available position, become restless, and leave as soon as a job at his level comes along.

Job seekers tend to complain about the "us" vs. "them" type of employee/employer relationship. But what they seem to forget is that most employers in this country are really no different in their attitudes and beliefs from the job seekers themselves. They are just on the other side of the desk with a different set of circumstances to deal with. Can we really blame the employer for choosing the individual most suited (read: evenly qualified) for the opening? Wouldn't you?

At any rate, it's a fact that appearing or being overqualified for a position is a problem. But it is a problem only because the job seeker has not properly targeted his market.

Several years ago I had a client who was a high-level, high-powered corporate attorney in charge of the legal affairs of one of the country's largest insurance companies. His salary was more than $300,000 per year. But that did not make him happy. What made him happy was his family, a group of people he saw only rarely. "It's not worth it. It's not worth any amount of money," he said to me one day. "I might as well be a prisoner who sends big checks to my family from jail. There's really little difference. My family enjoys life and I work."

My client figured he would be a bargain at *half* his salary (which was all he really needed). Then he could work a normal work week and get a new lease on life. Wrong! Believe it or not, no one wanted to hire someone who was willing to work for half his salary. No one trusted his reasons. Prospective employers felt there was some other reason for his willingness to relinquish $150,000 per year and much of his power. No one was more surprised about this attitude than my client. His problem, he finally realized, was within himself. He drove himself too hard. He set himself up for 100-hour weeks. He wouldn't delegate and relinquish control. Unless he changed, his environment never would.

So how do you handle the situation of being overqualified?

The answer is simple: Keep your focus on the highest level of your value and capability. *Don't compromise.* Put your very best points down on paper, but make that paper land in the hands of the audience that values those points. Find the wrong audience and you will get the wrong reaction. Spend the time to find the best markets, and also search for other markets that value the highest level of your experience, skills, and/or education. Follow the Winning Moves in this book. But don't ever compromise. For example, don't hide your advanced education because you think it will make you look overqualified for the position. You earned these honors. They show your value. Don't lower your level of achievement or number of accomplishments on the job.

If the prospective employer doesn't value your level of training, experience, and/or abilities, then their job is not the job for you.

No one has abilities, education, training, or experience that is *too good* for the job market. There is no ceiling in the job market. The problem, like the problem with my attorney client, is one that lies within the job seeker and his job search, not the job market.

So don't compromise. Compromise yourself and you will compromise your self-esteem. Compromise your self-esteem, and your job performance will be diminished. Diminish your job performance and you will lose the job. Lose the job and you will be back at square one, wondering why you took a job that was beneath you in the first place!

II

Marketing
Yourself

Think of Yourself as a Product with Value Rather Than a Person with Need

Years ago I went to a Boat Show in Boston, looking to buy a canoe. When I intently entered a booth where there were both canoes and high-speed powerboats, the salesman sensed that I was hot to buy. But he made one critical mistake. He didn't understand my needs and tried to sell me a powerboat. I patiently waited out his sales pitch, not wanting to be abrupt. But he'd already lost me. If he didn't care to understand my needs, I thought, why should I fulfill his?

Why do people buy a product? Because they see value in it. They see a benefit to themselves. When people hire people they too are buying a product, one in which they see value and benefit. You are the product. They are the market. What are the product's biggest benefits? What market has the greatest use for these benefits? Which market is the easiest to penetrate?

Simple. Identify your benefits. Look for the matching market to "consume" these benefits. Sell yourself to that market. Follow the Winning Moves in this section on marketing. They, like you, have value, and they will guide you along the path to the market. Stay on that path. Don't waste time on the wrong match. You'll use up valuable energy, which will generate negative feedback and lower your self-esteem—and ultimately your value as well.

21

And how do you determine your value in the job market? There are both general and very specific publications on compensation rates. The government's *Occupational Outlook Handbook,* found in most libraries, gives fairly general compensation information on nearly all professions. It's a good place to start.

For more detailed compensation information, look to professional societies and associations to find publications listing income by job function, level of education, level of experience, length of experience, professional status, number of people supervised, and work region. The National Society of Professional Engineers, for example, publishes yearly a highly detailed, 125-page professional engineer income and salary survey.

Contacting a leading association representing your industry is a good way to determine compensation rates. (See Winning Move #10 for more specific information on associations and how to find and contact them.)

Another way to determine compensation in your profession is to network with other professionals and specialized headhunters in your field. This approach will get you information that is more up to date, more local, and less standardized. (See Winning Moves #9, #12, and #39 for how to get the kind of information you need from your network and from headhunters.)

Some companies will pay according to what they perceive as your value to them. Others will have budgets and policies that are not flexible. Your previous salary may or may not have any bearing on what your compensation offer will be. If your past salary has been on the high side of the scale, it's possible that your value may appear higher. On the other hand, your prospective employer may not be able to afford you and may reject you because he feels you'll never be happy going backward. In short, there are too many variables to standardize the salary approach. Your best bet, as I've said before, is to do everything possible to find the best match between you, your skill level, and the company. Show your prospective employer how your particular background, special skills, innate abilities, and past contributions to other employers would make you an employee with special, added value. Then negotiate.

And remember the value of fringe benefits: They're a deduction for the company and an *after-tax* value to you, whereas your salary is *before tax.* So, in many cases it is in your better interest to negotiate benefits rather than salary.

It's Easier for Companies to Hire from Within— So Get Within

For a company to look outside itself for new people is more expensive, more time-consuming, and riskier than finding new candidates internally or within its network. Why should a company spend money on a headhunter or an expensive classified ad if they don't have to? Why should they trust an outsider? Going outside is the last recourse.

For years I had entry-level clients who insisted on following traditional channels to try to get radio jobs in Boston. Very few ever got anywhere. Finally I found out why. Almost all of the radio stations used a small, Boston-area college's School of Communications to feed them their people. It was all they needed and all they used. Everyone else was circular-filed.

Be Like an Eagle, Not Like a Buzzard: Buzzards Wait and Look for Remains, While Eagles Soar and Hunt Their Prey

How do you find out how companies find their new employees?

- One way is a simple telephone poll. In the case of the radio-station jobs, a polite, tactful telephone call to radio stations would have revealed a hiring pattern: "Hi, I'm interested in the field of broadcasting and I'm wondering if you would be kind enough to let me know how WXYZ goes about finding new people in this area." This usually gets a straight answer or at least a referral to someone who can give you one. "Kind enough," by the way, is an enormously effective phrase, appealing to a person's sense of decency. Use it often.

- Another method of determining hiring patterns is to call headhunters (professionals whose business it is to act as independent agents to find candidates for companies with job openings). You can obtain the names of the headhunters specializing in your industry or field through the comprehensive *Directory of Executive Recruiters*, published by Kennedy Publications in Fitzwilliam, New Hampshire. Call the headhunters in your geographical area; the directory breaks its listings down by state and industry specialization. Remember, headhunters are people who spend their days in the world of hiring for certain industries. They know about specific companies and their hiring procedures. They spend much of their time cold-calling companies to offer their services. Don't push them to find you a job—if they're interested, you can be sure they'll speak up—but gently probe them for information, flattering them a bit if you have to. You might say: "I read that you're a specialist in the area of media employment, and I'm wondering if you'd be kind enough to help me determine how major Boston radio stations find new employees."

- Another way to determine how particular companies find people is to call their human resources representative directly. Most companies with 100 or more employees have at least one professional dedicated to the human resources function. (The term "personnel" is passé—don't use it.) Directories of key human resources people are published by industry associations. For example, in New England, *The Northeast Human Resources Association* publishes the names and phone numbers of human resources people from more than 3,000 companies. Human resources people are hard to get to, but persistence will pay off with key information on how they hire. (See Winning Move #10 for more information on how to find association directories.)

- If you can't find the company you want in a professional directory, make a simple telephone call to the main switchboards of your target companies, saying: "I'm sending some correspondence to your Director of Human Resources, and I'm not certain of that person's name. Could you help me?" The response will vary, depending on the company's size. You may get the name of the Director, if they have such a position. Or the company may be so small that the person answering the phone says, "Well, Sally Jones, our Vice President, usually handles that sort of thing." Or, if they're *really* small, the response might be, "You've reached the Director, the President, the Operator, and the guy who empties the trash. What can I do for you?" At any rate, you'll get more market data to plug into your search on hiring.

Larger companies have job-posting or requisition systems, which often include company-published books of internal job orders. If you can network with someone inside the company, it may be possible to obtain a copy. Make a list of anyone you know who is remotely involved in your target industry, even if it's a friend of a friend of the uncle of your ex-wife. With tenacious networking (see Winning Move #12) you can get the inside scoop and, with luck, a copy of the job listings. Once you have this, and you can see a position that matches your qualifications or abilities, you can develop a strategy for approaching the appropriate human resources person (often a specialist called a company recruiter) with your specific job-matching qualifications. The company recruiter's job is to fill positions; it only makes sense for this person to want his or her job made easier.

If the right channels aren't filling the position, the recruiter wants the next-best, cheapest, and most expeditious solution. With this approach you can be on the "inside" even though you are technically on the outside of the company. By writing the recruiter, showing your knowledge of the position, and aligning your qualifications with the company's needs, you can most likely generate a meeting. You will appeal to the recruiter's needs, and provide a quick and easy solution to his or her job requisition. The "outside" job seekers will be left in the dust.

So get inside. Every company has its own system for hiring. Find it. Find someone who was hired and find out how he or she was found. Learn the company's culture from that person. Learn the kind of people the company likes and the way they like to be approached. And use the telephone; it's one of your strongest allies. It is cheap and brings you quick, bottom-line information.

Make Your Job Search 80 Percent Research

You are fortunate to be living in the greatest information era in history. Just about everything about anything can be found right down the street at your local library.

Let me take you through some examples. Let's say you're a marketing person and want to focus your job search on the toy industry. You'll need to get all of the available market information: (1) the future outlook of the industry, (2) the strengths and weaknesses of various companies within the industry, and (3) the key contacts at your area of penetration within each company. No problem. Begin by visiting your local library. Smile when you go in. Find the reference librarian—these people are wonderful and *love* to help find stuff. Here's a sample of what you'll uncover about the toy industry.

From the *Standard Industrial Classification Manual Index* (found in any library) you'll learn that there are seven toy-related categories:

5945 Toy and game stores—retail
3612 Toy transformers—mfg.
5092 Toys (including electronic)—wholesale
3942 Toys, doll—mfg.
3069 Toys, rubber: except dolls—mfg.
3942 Toys, stuffed—mfg.
3944 Toys: except dolls, bicycles, rubber toys,
     and stuffed toys—mfg.

Let's say your focus is on manufacturing stuffed toys. (You always loved your teddy bear and want to market those old faithful companions to children worldwide.) Here is what you'll find under 3942 Dolls & Stuffed Toys:

Total of 22 companies
Total sales of $666 million
Total employment: 6,600

Under companies (I'll show 4 of 22) you'll find the following information:

1. Tonka Corp., 6000 Clearwater Dr., Minnetonka, MN 55343. 612-936-3300. Public. $908M sales.
2. Russ Berrie & Co., Inc., 111 Bauer Dr., Oakland, NJ 07436. 201-337-9000. Public. $276M sales.
3. Applause, Inc., P.O. Box 4183, Woodland Hills, CA 91365. 818-992-6000. Privately held. $98M sales.
22. Dollcraft Industries, Ltd., 1107 Broadway, New York, NY 10010. 212-807-7933. Privately held. $1M sales.

Let's start at the top, at the biggest—Tonka. If you look under Tonka Corporation in the *Directory of Corporate Affiliations* (Section 2—Parent Companies), you'll find:

Tonka Corporation, Minnetonka Corporate Center, 6000 Clearwater Dr., Minnetonka, MN 55343. 612-936-3300
(also fax and telex numbers)
Assets: $910M
Earnings: $5,800,000 [oh oh—losing money!]
Liabilities: $822M [oh oh—debt!]
Net worth: $88M
Approximate sales: $908M
Employees: 3,600
Manufacturer of toys and games

The directory goes on to list corporate officers, from Chairman down to Vice President of Marketing and Product Development, and then their operating units: Tonka International and Parker

Brothers in Beverly, Massachusetts, Tonka Products Division in Minnetonka, Minnesota, and Kenner Products Division in Cincinnati, Ohio.

"Gee," you say, "it's a big company. There should be lots of hiring and a place for me." But first you'll want to learn even more details about Tonka's products and financial standing. You can find it in *Moody's Industrial Manual* in your local library. This provides 15 years of Tonka's stock performance, and accounts of recent developments, such as: "On January 31, 1991, Hasbro agreed to purchase Tonka for $470 million. For the quarter ended 9/30/90, net income dropped 62.5% . . . ." Ah ha!! Will Hasbro be cleaning house at Tonka? Will they bring in their own people? Perhaps this is a good time to approach Hasbro with your skills rather than Tonka? Certainly Tonka Corporation does not appear to be the right avenue. You read on about Tonka: "Mired with debt from the 1987 acquisition of Kenner Parker and a sluggish retail environment, the near-term earnings outlook is weak. Also, Tonka has been unable to come up with any hot new toys."

You can go still further. *Value Line Investment Survey*, in the section titled Ratings and Reports, tells you that "the toy industry experienced a soft retail environment during the second quarter. But one company which continues to do well is Mattel, which posted increases in both sales and earnings for the period."

So on you go to Mattel, and then others, repeating the process outlined above until you find the hottest prospects with the best hiring potential and financial futures.

To learn still more about the toy industry, you can go on to the *Encyclopedia of Business Information Sources*, 7th edition. Here you'll find detailed industry information on:

- *Specialized directories within the toy industry.* Example: *The Official Toy Trade Directory*, Edgell Communications, 545 Fifth Avenue, New York, NY 10017. 212-503-2913. $8.00.
- *On-line data bases.* Many mid-sized to large libraries have a computerized search system such as InfoTrac or CompuServe. For a minimal cost, you can log on to obtain specific information. Your reference librarian will be glad to help you plug in a key search phrase. The computer will then scan various media materials to give you sources of

information around your key phrase. These data bases are
useful, and they're getting more sophisticated all the time.
The *Encyclopedia of Business Information Sources* tells us,
for example, that there's an on-line data base on a U.S.
Census on retail trade, something that could tell us about
the prognosis of retail sales in the United States.

- *Statistics sources.* Example: *U.S. Industrial Outlook*, which
  says: "Strong import competition and the continued
  movement of domestic manufacturers to off-shore production
  sites kept toy industry employment down in 1989.
  Domestic corporations continued to shift production to Far
  East markets to take advantage of lower labor costs.
  Increasingly, the domestic toy industry is more involved with
  the licensing, marketing, packaging, and distribution of
  dolls, toys, and games."

Hmm. U.S. manufacturing of toys is not good, they say; it's
going overseas. But marketing is growing domestically. And you're
in marketing. Let's see what the trade associations, professional
societies, and trade periodicals have to say.

- *Trade associations and professional societies.* These are great
  sources of information. For a nominal charge you can join
  one of them and gain access to current industry information,
  sub-groups, industry networking meetings, specialized
  industry training, and very detailed directories. Many
  associations even provide their own industry job listing
  service. You learn that the Toy Manufacturers of America
  Association is located on Fifth Avenue in New York City.
- *Periodicals and newsletters.* From these publications, the names
  of which you can find from such sources as the
  *Encyclopedia of Business Information Sources, The Directory
  of Directories* and *The Newsletter on Newsletters,* you
  can get more specific information on particular products, on
  trends, and on smaller, non-public organizations. You'll find
  such a title as *Playthings: The News Magazine of Toy, Hobby
  and Craft Merchandising.* There could be good stuff in
  here. If there are articles pertinent to your interests in toy
  marketing, you'll gain further industry knowledge, help
  your job search, and ultimately gain more credibility.

Further, networking with the authors of articles can be a superb job-search tool. Write the authors of the articles that interest you, flatter the writers, ask intelligent questions, and develop relationships with these people. If you do this well, you'll eventually get yourself some much-needed inside information and contacts, working yourself closer to the coveted hidden market of toy industry hiring.

Finally, trade magazine advertisements will give you clues and information on specialized products within the industry, and on the emerging smaller firms of which little or nothing is written in the library publications. For example, in *Playthings*, you might see a trade ad that tells of a fast-growing stuffed-bear product, distributed by an emerging firm in New York City, not far from your home in Pelham, New York. You call the company and explain that you read their trade ad in *Playthings*, and found their stuffed-bear product very appealing. You ask if you could speak to someone involved in the marketing of the product. From this person you learn that the company is small, and primarily an importer, marketing their product here in the States. They could be just the company you are looking for.

Like underground streams, the information and the smaller, less prominent companies are there, gurgling away. And these companies are vital, more flexible, more dynamic, more exciting, and no less secure than many of the well-known giants. Dig deep. Don't give up. And you'll be rewarded long before your fellow job seekers.

The Bibles of Job-Search Research

Standard Industrial Classification Manual Index
Directory of Corporate Affiliations
Moody's Industrial Manual
Value Line Investment Survey: Ratings and Reports
Encyclopedia of Business Information Sources
U.S. Industrial Outlook
Encyclopedia of Associations
The Directory of Directories

Get Them to Want You Before They Need You

Imagine you are an inexperienced, unskilled salesperson given the job of selling air-purification systems in a region within a 15-mile radius of Boston. This is probably what you would do:

Walk out of your office with your product and its literature and knock on the door of the next office.

Explain to the person who opens the door that you're selling air-purification systems.

Hope that you can demonstrate the product and close the sale.

Go on to the office next door and repeat the process.

Now imagine you are a skilled sales veteran given the job of selling air-purification systems within the same region. This is probably what you would do:

Develop a complete understanding of the key benefits of the
air-purification system you're selling.

Define the particular audience within your region that is most
likely to benefit from those key benefits (this is called
your *target market*).

Structure an approach to this audience that most effectively
and efficiently communicates the value of the product's
key benefits to the target audience.

Implement your approach in a manner that is time-efficient
and allows you full opportunity for proper follow-through.

Notice the difference? The skilled salesperson puts in significant research and development time *before* he or she walks out of
the home office. In the long run, this actually saves considerable
effort, which would otherwise have been wasted pitching (and
usually losing) unqualified prospects. The skilled sales veteran's
targeted approach, by yielding a more positive response and greater
return, not only does not waste his effort, but it increases his
motivation and conviction that the product has appeal and will sell.
This makes the job of selling much easier.

Now think about what you are doing for a moment. You are a
job seeker. You want to demonstrate your talents, skills, and/or
abilities to a particular employer. You want to communicate your
benefit to potential companies. In essence, you are a human product
with certain benefits who is looking for a buyer. You are a salesperson selling yourself.

Think about yourself and your profession. Answer the following
questions: What is it you do? What is the title of what you do? What
type of industry do you best do it in? What geographical area will
you do it in?

Sell Yourself to Them Before They
Realize They Have to Come to You

By just waiting for people to announce their need for you
through advertised job openings, you are only tapping into what I
call the reactive market. That is the market that already has an

opening. It does not cover the market that will have *upcoming* openings. Just as the skilled air-purification system salesperson would not go about selling his product by just waiting for people to call him, you need to sell yourself to the market that has the potential to hire you.

Let's follow Sam Gilford, a staff accountant who takes a proactive approach in his job search. After eight years, Sam's employer, a $22-million manufacturing firm, laid him off. After several months in a job-search program consisting only of responding to help-wanted ads, Sam knew he had to try a different approach.

Sam was frustrated because he knew there had to be more staff accountant positions open than those he'd seen advertised. He'd read a statistic that said most positions turned over in three years or less. If that was so, where were they? And he'd heard about the "hidden job market," which told him that most jobs are filled before they have to be advertised. In fact, he'd read somewhere that help-wanted advertisements accounted for only about one-tenth of the hiring market, and that most employers know of impending openings between 30 and 90 days before they actually take action to fill them. He figured he had to get to the positions while the openings were brewing—*before* they were actively being filled.

So Sam developed an approach that accomplished the following:

- It defined his target region and market. (See Winning Move #10 to learn how to research your target region and market.)
- It defined his target audience.
- It gave him the selling tools he needed.
- It gave him a statistical understanding of his potential rate of return, which allowed him to understand his odds.
- It gave him something tangible and proactive to do instead of just waiting.
- It gave him hope.
- It generated a larger network and enhanced his knowledge of the job market in his field.

Here's what Sam's job-search marketing plan looked like:

Product	Sam Gilford, staff accountant for a mid-sized manufacturing firm in the Boston area
Benefit	Eight years of broad-based, successful experience as a staff accountant in a mid-sized manufacturing firm
Target region	15-mile radius of Boston
Target market	200 manufacturing firms with $10–$100 million in sales
Target contact	Controller
Average number of staff accountant positions within this size manufacturing firm	2
Average turnover for staff accountants in this type of firm	Every 3 years
Average yield of position openings	11 openings every month!

Sam arrived at the above average yield figures through simple calculations:

$$200 \times 2 \div 36 = 11$$

Translation:

200 (target employers) $\times$ 2 (staff accountant positions per firm) = 400 positions. 400 positions divided by 36 months (3-year average turnover in each position) = 11 positions opening per month.

Best of all, the above figuring gave Sam a sense that there was light at the end of the tunnel that was his job search. Statistically, he now knew that every month he had a chance to land one of nearly a dozen job openings within his field and region. He now had a clear-cut plan with targets to shoot at. Enacting the plan wouldn't be fun, but it would be productive, and it would bring him closer to his goal. If nothing came from these 200 firms, he'd then try another 200 within a larger region. The path was long but clear. Suddenly there was hope.

Sam knew he now needed to find the names, addresses, and key contacts within each of the 200 target firms. He went to his town library and set up a meeting with the reference librarian. He told the librarian his situation and what he wanted to accomplish. He was advised to start with a publication called the *Directory of Massachusetts Manufacturers*. (See Winning Move #10 for more information on researching companies.) The directory, through a classification called an SIC (Standard Industrial Code), gave him valuable product-by-product information within the manufacturing field in Massachusetts. The directory was also broken down by cities and towns, which made it easy for Sam to stay within his target area. Just on one page for one large town, Sam found four manufacturers that fit his target. And there were more than 100 other towns within his 15-mile target area! The directory gave him valuable information such as computer system, gross sales, number of employees, product or products manufactured, and the names of key contacts in management. It even gave each company's main telephone number, which was the next thing he needed, because he had some telephoning to do.

After Sam compiled his list, he allocated some job-search time to calling each number and obtaining the name of each company's controller, his target contact.

This is what he said:

"Good morning, my name is Sam Gilford, and I'm scheduled to be forwarding some correspondence to your accounting department. Could I please have the name of your controller?"

Sam found that the vast majority of the companies he called had no problem giving out the names he needed. His list was really taking shape! He had key names within key target companies.

Sam had to develop his approach. First, he wrote down his assets to remind himself why he was already ahead of his competition.

Assets
I'm already ahead of my competition because I'm bypassing human resources and I have identified the individual who is likely to feel the greatest need for my skills and capabilities. Except for internal applicants, this will get me as close to the inside track as possible for upcoming positions.

Then he listed what he expected to be his obstacles and how he might overcome them.

Obstacles
The Controller doesn't know me from a hole in the wall. Therefore I need to get his attention. And I need to show value. I can't look like just another person needing a job.

Remedy
Develop a strong "broadcast" letter, an unsolicited letter sent to key contacts, which:
 • gets read
 • is as personalized as possible
 • is value-oriented
 • makes it easy for me to follow up

Next, Sam went about developing his broadcast letter. See the finished product, ready to be mailed, on the next page.

Samuel R. Gilford
3 Collard Lane
Middleton, MA 01949
(508) 777-0984

January 8, 1994

Harold Gomes
Controller
Eastern Canvas Products Inc.
50 Rogers Road
Haverhill, MA 01830

Dear Mr. Gomes:

Eastern Canvas may be able to benefit from my solid experience as a staff accountant within a major manufacturing firm.

My strength and benefit to you is in my ability to effectively and efficiently handle a broad range of manufacturing accounting functions, including: payroll, accounts receivable and payable, cash disbursements, sales, and excise and quarterly tax returns.

I am comfortable with computerized systems, including IBM minis and PCs running Lotus and a variety of customized and off-the-shelf accounting packages.

I have a proven ability to apply both systems and procedures that can reduce the burden and cost of your corporate accounting functions.

I can provide the highest level of professional recommendations.

Mr. Gomes, regardless of whether or not you have a position at the moment, I'd very much like to discuss Eastern Canvas's needs and my own ability to add value to your staff should the opportunity arise in the future. I'll plan on giving you a call next week to see if we might get together. Perhaps I might buy you lunch.

Sincerely yours,

Samuel R. Gilford

Sam's letter is excellent for a number of reasons:

- It is personalized and does not threaten or hard-sell Mr. Gomes.
- It is short enough to be read easily.
- It lists industry skills that are most likely to be relevant to the needs of the reader.
- It does not ask for a job, only for a chance to share ideas and show potential for mutual benefit.
- It includes a free lunch. (Remember, if you bring forth offerings, people will talk to you.)
- Finally and importantly, it does not include a résumé! Sam did this intentionally because he felt that sending just a personalized letter would keep his relationship closer. *A letter without a résumé changes the tone away from "I'm looking for work" to one of "We should get to know one another."* Further, it would be hard for Mr. Gomes to forward a personalized letter (with no résumé) to human resources. And it would be hard for Mr. Gomes to throw away a letter that was thoughtful and asked for the courtesy of a response from an upcoming telephone call. Besides, Sam knew that even if Mr. Gomes wanted a résumé at the point of his follow-up telephone call, he would still be ahead of the game, having his foot partway in the door simply because he had Mr. Gomes's ear.

Sam sent this letter and nine others out on a Wednesday. On Friday he sent another ten, and on the following Wednesday he sent ten more, in addition to following up by telephone on his first mailing. His goal was to repeat this cycle until he'd sent out and followed up on all 200 letters. Needless to say, Sam's life as a job seeker suddenly became quite full. His day was broken up into research (he did what research he could on each company, and then spliced whatever knowledge he gained into his broadcast letter to increase its impact), broadcast letter writing and mailing, telephone follow-up, appointments, and lunches.

Follow Up on Everything!

How much insurance would you sell if you waited for your prospects to call you back to order?

Sam's telephone follow-ups directly to his key contacts were more difficult than his earlier calls, when all he'd needed from the company was the Controller's name. Now he actually needed to take some of the key contact's time, and he often found his path blocked, usually in the form of his key contact's secretary.

In the case of his follow-up with Mr. Gomes at Eastern Canvas, Sam encountered his secretary, Ms. Shuman. But Sam was clever and approached it like this:

Sam: *(voice very friendly)* Hi! Who's this?

Ms. Shuman: This is Ms. Shuman.

Sam: *(self-assured)* Ms. Shuman, this is Sam Gilford. Is Mr. Gomes in?

Ms. Shuman: Ah, yes, I believe so. What is this regarding?

Sam: I sent him some materials I said I'd be following up on.

[call transfer]

Sam: Mr. Gomes, this is Sam Gilford from Middleton calling. *(no pause)* I sent you a letter last week outlining how I might be of value to Eastern Canvas in your accounting department.

Mr. Gomes: Yes, Sam, I did have a look at your letter. Your background looks interesting, but, I tell you, I'm tied up at the moment and besides . . .

Sam: *(interrupting so as not to encounter a "no")* No problem. I just wanted to touch base to see if you received my letter. Could I check back tomorrow? Any special time?

[They agreed that Sam would follow up with a telephone call the next morning.]

[Next morning]

Sam: (*self-assured*) Ms. Shuman, this is Sam Gilford. Mr. Gomes asked me to call him this morning. May I speak to him, please?

Ms. Shuman: One moment, please, Mr. Gilford.

[call transfer]

Sam: Mr. Gomes, this is Sam Gilford from Middleton calling you back as you asked.

Mr. Gomes: Oh, yes, Sam, I did have a look again at your letter. But it's been hectic around here. Refresh my memory a bit. What did you have in mind?

Sam: Well, as an experienced staff accountant coming from a manufacturing environment, I feel particularly well equipped to serve on the staff of someone such as yourself. Actually, I'm pretty good at making things less hectic in the accounting area! I just felt that, regardless of whether you need someone like me at the moment, I could give you a sense of my capabilities and perhaps a few ideas I've brought along from Brewer & James Manufacturing.

Mr. Gomes: Well, you caught me right in the middle of this damn... Say, have you had any experience with these doggone interactive accounting/MIS packages?

[BINGO!!]

Sam: As a matter of fact, I have. With Brewer & James I...

Mr. Gomes: Well, then, send me your résumé and I'll take a look and get back to you.

[psst.—no, he won't!]

Sam: That's fine, but if you've any situations you'd like to bounce off me right away, I've got some good ideas you might find interesting. Maybe we could talk shop over lunch? Besides, at that point I can further detail my background as it would fit your needs.

Mr. Gomes: Well, things are pretty tight—we're trying to keep costs down. You know how it is.

Sam: Sure. I can understand where you're coming from. I've been there myself. But I think if you share with me some of your objectives and we talk shop, I might be able to give you some of my ideas, which, whether you use me or not, could be of benefit. Besides, I'll buy—it's a free lunch. Sort of a win-win situation!

Mr. Gomes: Well, maybe you're right. Friday's a possibility.

[You're rolling now, Sam!]

After a productive luncheon meeting with Mr. Gomes the following Friday, Sam feels good. Regardless of whether Mr. Gomes hires him, through his face-to-face meeting Sam has accomplished the following:

- He's planted a seed for future employment with Eastern Canvas.
- He's gotten to know a Controller who can refer him to other Controllers who may need staff accountants.
- He's gained more informational interviewing experience as well as specialized knowledge about what other manufacturers want in a staff accountant.

But there's little time to dwell on the results of that meeting. He knows his odds of success in the job hunt will continually increase with each contact he makes. And Sam has a list of 199 companies to approach! That will add up to a lot of contacts. And better odds with each one.

Winning Move #12:

Use a Network to
Catch Your Prey

Statistics tells us that 85 percent of all jobs are never advertised. Rather, they are circulated—and filled—through an inside "network." This network is made up of individuals who, quite simply, are the most immediately accessible—not necessarily the most qualified—for the upcoming job opening. If you are a job hunter who is not networking, you are missing 85 percent of the job market. You are competing with every other job hunter for a mere 15 percent of the total openings in the employment marketplace. Not good odds!

By the Time a Hot Job Reaches the Newspapers, It's Usually Too Late

Ask yourself this question: If you could choose to interview an applicant who has been referred to you by a colleague or a perfect stranger, with whom would you rather talk?

Networking is a cumulative activity. It is a delicate science, a weaving of interconnected contacts. When properly done, it can maximize your best asset: the people who know your value. Begin with the people nearest to you—friends, family members, business associates with whom you've established a personal relationship. Each of these people will have a set of contacts who may be of use to you. People are willing to lend a hand because it feels good to help. It's in their nature to give advice and make recommendations. So as a networker you have this in your favor. People who know you and believe in you will most likely *want* to recommend you. But recommend you for what and to whom? And will they say the right thing? And is their reputation a positive one? Do they really know what you want?

Your Network Needs to Be Spoon-fed Ever So Carefully

As a networker, you need to nourish and nurture each contact in your network. Unfortunately, that is not what usually happens. Here is an example of bad (and typical) networking.

You lose your job as Administrative Services Manager at Typicorp. You're mad as hell and understandably frazzled, but figure you had better not waste any time. That's your first mistake. You immediately call Colleen Smith, a contact in Administrative Services at Acme, Inc., a competitor. Colleen once indicated at a trade show that she liked your style. And now, on the phone, Colleen seems sympathetic, so you give her an earful, saying how shortsighted Typicorp was in eliminating such a valuable position as yours. Further, you continue, Typicorp was not the place to be anyway; you really always wanted to be with a progressive company like Acme, Inc. Did she have anything?

Great speech, you think, she may just jump at the opportunity.

But Colleen's reaction is just the opposite.

First, she feels as if she and Acme, Inc., are a second choice, a fallback for you. She feels used. She hasn't heard from you in months. Now you've got problems and you unload them on her.

Second, Colleen feels your anger, and that just makes her uncomfortable.

Third, she doesn't like the fact that, not even one full day after being let go from your company, you are suddenly bad-mouthing Typicorp. Wouldn't you be capable of doing the same to Acme, Inc.?

Finally, and ironically, she really made that trade show comment about liking your style as a part of her own networking, to plant seeds for possible opportunities at Typicorp, in case anything went awry at Acme, Inc.! Now, in light of your comments about Typicorp, she thinks she'll happily stay put. In fact, she'll do everything she can to protect her position.

Proper Networking: Guidelines for Launching Your Networking Effort

Give Yourself Time to Vent Any Anger

If you have to unload, do it on someone who's close to you, who can't or won't harm your job search, and who can both empathize and offer objective advice. Sometimes a well-reputed career counselor can also help, but don't blindly hire one. Get references or ask around.

Taking your anger, hurt, or diminished self-esteem directly into the face of your most valuable contacts is a serious mistake. Give yourself a few days to recompose. During those days, concentrate on making a list of your value points, skills, and career/job achievements, rather than focusing on the negatives of your situation. *Look backward only if it brings you ahead.*

Make a Three-column List of Your Network

In the left-hand column of a large sheet of paper, list your contacts or any contacts of contacts. These should be people who, for whatever reason, know your skills and/or industry, have valuable connections or contacts in your industry or the new field into which you are headed, or can connect you to valuable contacts.

Make your list as exhaustive as possible; sleep on it; tap into the mental data bases of other people for names that have slipped your mind (you'll be amazed at some of the obvious contacts you've temporarily forgotten). Review any industry memos, notes, association lists, or trade publications to jog your memory for names you may have ignored. Look into your situation with a historical perspective: What did your previous colleagues do when they were in your situation? Which contacts worked? Which ones didn't? Where did your old colleagues finally land?

In the second column, list the relationship of these names to you and your industry or field of interest.

In the third column, comment on what they could possibly do for you, and/or whom they might contact on your behalf.

An example would look like this:

John Short	Met at '92 sales conference in Chicago. He's a distributor for Widget Molds.	Knows distributor network and most key players; seemed to have pulse of the industry.
Bob Ambrose	Met at Saab dealership (we both bought red Saabs). He used to be in my industry.	Knows Schwartz, Sr. VP - Execumold - a major player. He must have GREAT contacts.
Colleen Smith	Met at Widget Fare '91 trade show.	Works in Administrative Services at Acme, Inc., a competitor. She "liked my style."

Make a File Folder for Each Name

Label the folder and make a data sheet for each name, restating the information on that individual. You now have something tangible, something to work with in your job search. You have a stack of folders (leads!) ready to accumulate information relative to your job search. Suddenly there appears to be much more to work with than just the Sunday classifieds.

Now Make a Second Sheet

On it outline the best approach and best time of approach for each name on the list. Ask yourself questions about the logic of approaching each contact: Is this a bad time to contact him since it's his most hectic season? Would I be stepping on his toes by first contacting her rather than him? Is a lunch appropriate? Should I write a note first? To pave the way, what about that industry article I found interesting? Maybe I should send it to Colleen to break the ice—I haven't seen her in a while and it could smooth the way to talk about Acme, Inc.

Get a Large Calendar of the Current Month

Transfer the dates planned for your initial contact and/or correspondence with each person from each folder. You'll be surprised at how full your calendar will suddenly become. For example, if you have 30 names, you will have at least 30 things to do. These 30 tasks will be either letters, phone calls, or personal calls to approach your network. When accomplished correctly, these 30 tasks will blossom into more tasks: lunches, informational interviews, more letters and phone calls to new names referred from the initial contacts. As you can see, the goal here is to nourish each contact, to allow it to bloom and create further contacts, hence enlarging your network, increasing your odds, and bringing you closer to your ultimate goal: the right job.

Understand the Do's and Don'ts of Approaching and Activating Your Network.

- Contact each person in your network in a way that is the most convenient and least imposing for that person.
- Approach each contact in the most complimentary way possible. *Examples:* "Everyone I spoke to said if anybody might know about this it would be you."—"Jim, you know a lot of people and I have lots to offer. I know they'd value

your comments about my abilities."—"Everyone said you were the guru."—"I'd respect your ideas and opinions on where I might go next in the area of..."—"I've got what I think are some good ideas regarding...and I'd really value your feedback."

- Be respectful of your contact's time limitations.
- Clearly communicate as specifically as possible what you do, why you are good, and where you best do what you're good at!
- Don't say something like: "I'd appreciate it if you'd let me know if you hear of anything that opens up in my area." This request will get limited or no response. The contact person won't know what specific task is assigned to him or her, and therefore probably won't take any specific action.
- Give each contact a specific task, not a general one. Then the contact can take action. *Examples:* "Would you know of any individuals within that division with whom I might speak? If I check back on Friday, could I get those names from you?"—"I'm trying to learn more about the profile of management candidates in your field. Could you be kind enough to tell me what kinds of people you like to hire?"
- Don't say you need a job. Don't ask for a job. Don't bad-mouth anyone.
- Don't approach your most powerful contacts right away. Develop your learning curve and make your mistakes on what you think are your least-valuable contacts. Accumulate as much information as possible before presenting yourself to the critical and most powerful contacts in your network.

Networking is a very natural human response to any situation of need. Networking is something you do nearly every day. You tap into other people's mental data banks to connect with valuable information or people. You do it naturally. You do it when you need to know the name of a good restaurant. You do it when your car brakes need a good repair person. You do it when you need a good physician.

If You Don't Have the Contacts,
Make Them!

And you should do it when you are job seeking. Just as you would naturally indicate what kind of restaurant or what kind of a car or what kind of doctor you need, in job-search networking you should indicate what kind of job you want. Job-search networking, however, requires more effort than most other kinds of networking. It requires preparation and forethought, prior to the contact-making. The contacts are often more critical, and in shorter supply. The whole process is more precious and needs to be treated that way, because precious things, by their very nature, are of great value.

III

Selling
Yourself

Even If You Are the Queen of England, the Pope, or Lee Iacocca, Keep Your Résumé to One Page!

A résumé is a snapshot of your qualifications as they match the needs of a particular position. And a snapshot is one thing, not two. Your résumé's only goal is to prove that you're worth the time that an interview takes. It will have to communicate your value points and experience within 20 to 30 seconds. If it asks the reader for more time, it may instead get time in the wastebasket.

Your Résumé Is Usually Read by a Stranger About a Stranger

The reader's interest level is often low as the page is unfolded; it is even lower as two pages are unfolded. In this day of junk mail and paper overload, the reading, not to mention the assimilation, of two pages of single-spaced text is a rare occurrence, even a phenomenon. Page two rarely gets read because readers know that the older, less-pertinent information resides there. Also many readers feel that if you can't say it on one page, you are not a concise

55

communicator. Why run the risk of encountering one of these two-page résumé haters when you won't alienate anyone with one page.

You may be thinking: "But I have twenty-five years of experience in the field. How could I possibly put all that on one page? It's an injustice!" Sorry. On paper, you are more interesting to yourself than you ever will be to anyone else. Besides, the reader rarely cares about in-depth details of your early career years. Your most recent years usually are most important, and need description. For example, if you are now General Manager at Ace Gear Company, a detailed description of your prior years as Assistant Manager, Manager Trainee, and Clerk won't be of interest to the reader. You need only show that you advanced through these levels and list key accomplishments in these positions.

Build your résumé the way a skilled writer would build a short story, with every word playing an essential role toward communicating the story's central message. Any superfluous words will weaken the power of the message. If you force yourself to think about the value and connotation of *each word* you put down, you'll build a résumé with integrity. You'll build a résumé that makes a strong, cohesive, focused, one-page statement about why you're worth interviewing. If something in your background is obvious, irrelevant, or pulls the reader the wrong way, leave it out! If you are in doubt, ask yourself the question: "Does putting this in strengthen my case in any way?"

Give the reader an appetite for meeting you. A good one-page résumé will leave the reader with just enough of a taste to be hungry for more, rather than with a case of two-page indigestion.

They'll Ask Four Questions of Your Résumé—Make Sure You Have the Answers

Answering the following four questions in a fully persuasive way will greatly increase your odds of developing a winning résumé. These questions are the crucial elements of the résumé formula. Answering them will not only give you the material you need for building a strong résumé but will also prepare you for networking and interviewing.

Question #1: What do you want?

That's your *Objective*. Don't struggle or agonize over this. It's a simple question to which employers want a simple, specific answer. The most common objectives are the most damaging. *Example:* "To obtain a challenging, growth-oriented position within a dynamic organization that can utilize my skills." What did that say about what position you want? Nothing. Skip the gobbledygook. Besides, who doesn't want a challenging, growth-oriented position in a dynamic company? Would anyone want the opposite: a boring, dead-end position in a failing company? Tell them what you want as it fits what you feel they need. Change your objective for different markets, if you have to—it's not a problem with today's word-processing technology.

Examples of objectives:

Administrative Assistant, Marketing Department.
"C" Language Computer Programmer.
Head Nurse.
Elementary Teacher.
Senior Auditor.

And your Objective section doesn't need to say what type of organization you want. They know that. You sent the résumé to them!

Question #2: Why are you qualified to do it?

That's the *Summary* or *Qualifications* section. Answer, in succinct form, why you're qualified to accomplish your objective. That should be simple. Ask yourself why they should hire you. (You'll need to get ready for that one at the interview anyway!) Summarize the answer. You might say:

- Seven years of direct experience in...
- Extensive relevant study and degree in...
- Comprehensive knowledge of pertinent regulations of...
- Recognized leader in district performance for...
- Significant technical capabilities in...

These points become your Summary or Qualifications section (call it either). They prove you warrant your Objective. When done properly, this section satisfies the readers that the rest of your résumé is worth reading, bringing them to the next question.

Question #3: Where have you done it?

That's the *Experience* section. The reader wants to relate to the experience you've had. Identify the company in its most relevant light. If it's not a recognizable company, write a line about its high points. Build it up. On the résumé, the reader will often equate your value with that of your employer. Example:

Notknown Corporation, Boston, MA, a fast-emerging company in the field of plastic extrusions, with 35% yearly growth and numerous Fortune 1000 accounts.

Question #4: How well have you done it?

That's the *Achievement* section. This is where you should put in your most thought and effort. Think about what you did for each employer to make that company better. It could be a big thing or something small. But it should be enough to show value. Did you have an idea that was implemented and has saved the company money? Were you promoted several times as a result of consistent contributions? Were you given highly rated reviews, and why? Were you selected out of numerous employees for a key program or training? Bullet these points separately from and after your job description:

Recruiting Manager—Technical Temporaries (1987–present)
Direct overall operations of two locations, maintaining full sales, P&L, and budget responsibility ($12–$16 million). Hire, train, and manage section managers and staff. Review productivity of each section to maintain positive fill ratio, increase in percentage of markup, and a steady flow of qualified applicants/clients. Initiate and coordinate the recruiting of qualified applicants. Establish and maintain tracking mechanisms. Prepare and evaluate ongoing training programs in sales and recruiting areas with managers and sales reps.

Key Achievements:

- Took charge of an eroding $11-million division, and, in concert with sales manager, increased sales to $14 million in 12 months. Sales increased each month for 13 months over prior period.
- Direct a division that has billed up to 18,000 hours/week and sent more than 500 applicants out on assignment on a weekly basis.
- Initiated an industry-first technical training program that enhances our clients' marketability and verifies their skills.
- Built and retained a 22-person recruiting staff with very low turnover.

Winning Move #15:

Get Someone Else to Talk About You—It's Ten Times Better Than Talking About Yourself

Of course, you can say all you want about yourself in your résumé, but it's still *you* who's doing the talking about you. This is unsettling because, no matter how factual your summary, it still appears as a self-assessment and can be tough for the reader to swallow. The only outside reinforcement of your abilities comes from that one weak line: "References Available Upon Request." Since you're not asked to produce references until after the interview, this impotent line does little and takes up valuable space at the bottom of your résumé.

Don't despair! You can bring the power of "written legitimacy" to your résumé. If someone else for whom you've worked has written highly of your performance, splice it into the résumé. It will empower that piece of paper almost to the point of self-propulsion! It catches the reader's attention. It's very rarely done (I think I invented the idea). And it works! It works because someone else in a position to know is saying you're great.

Example:

JANE M. JOHNSON
3 Loring Avenue
Boston, MA 02107
(617) 264-1159

SUMMARY: Highly experienced sales professional with extensive background and achievements with a major Fortune 500 corporation, applying both sales and related administrative skills successfully in very challenging, competitive environments.

"Jane is constantly setting the standards by which all others are judged. She displays a zest and enthusiasm for her job that is contagious to the rest of us. To Jane there is nothing that cannot be accomplished."
10/2/91 RJR/Nabisco Performance Review

Notice how the quotation jumps out at the reader. It lends legitimacy to the previous part of the summary. Any actual review from most any level of colleague will work. And it will work with any vocation or industry, whether you're a teacher, nurse, salesperson, technician, college student, or whatever. Use it quick while the concept is still hot!

Smooth the Wrinkles Out of Your Background: The Most Common Résumé Dilemmas, and What to Do When:

16. Your Employment Chronology Works Against You

If your current or most recent job is not relevant to your objective, don't feel you have to put it first. Don't feel locked in by having to stick to the "reverse-chronology rule" of résumé writing. This was the mistake John Jones made with his first résumé (see page 64). His objective was a purchasing position, but he hadn't been in purchasing since 1989. Yet, because of the reverse-chronology rule, he felt he was supposed to place his most recent job first.

JOHN JONES' FIRST RÉSUMÉ

JOHN JONES
152 Elm Street
Swampscott, MA 01907
(617) 595-1556

OBJECTIVE: To obtain a position in Purchasing.

EXPERIENCE:
1990–Present

Marblehead Marine Services   Marblehead, MA
Responsible **Head Rigger** position requires staff supervision, record keeping (time and supply use for billing), and rigging operations for approximately 800 boats per year.

Interact with a wide range of MMS customers, both commercial and pleasure boat owners and operators.

Other responsibilities have included: . . .

1979–1989

Bank of Boston   Boston, MA
Promoted through several positions of increasing responsibility, including:

Senior Buyer/Assistant Purchasing Officer
Managed the procurement of general bank supplies, including materials-handling equipment, check-processing equipment, security/protection equipment, numerous printed forms used both externally and internally, and paper products for all locations. Also served as sole procurement representative in the Bank's Canton facility, responsible for all purchasing requirements for 700+ staff (excepting furniture and contracts).

Exemplary	
Achievements:	• Researched, developed, and instituted a corporation-wide contract for copy paper (130 million sheets). Negotiated firm pricing for nine months. *Result:* savings of $90,000 for 1990. (System still in place today.)

The problem with John's first résumé was that it set a tone that said: "This man is a marine services person who *used* to be a purchasing professional." Readers became prejudiced if their eyes first landed on "Head Rigger" before they read of John's professional career and capabilities in purchasing. They felt he had slipped off his career path. Because of the structure of the résumé, it was obvious that John's most recent experience was not purchasing experience. John's purchasing experience, therefore, didn't get the attention it deserved. And his first résumé didn't get him interviews.

John needed a way to counteract this and put the reader in the right frame of mind. See John's new résumé on page 66.

Notice what has changed:

- His new objective now ties in "purchasing" with the words "continue," "progressive," and "successful," bringing a sense of continuity to his situation.
- His new summary section focuses the reader on his purchasing capabilities and experience, thereby setting the right tone and supporting his ability to meet his Objective.
- Directly after the summary, John's new résumé keeps the reader on track by first listing his past purchasing experience under the new category Direct Experience. John doesn't alienate the reader by breaking the reverse-chronology rule because he has clearly labeled this as Direct Experience (he could also have labeled the category Relevant Experience). It is clear that John has kept the readers' needs in mind by putting his most relevant experience first.

JOHN JONES' NEW RÉSUMÉ

JOHN JONES
152 Elm Street
Swampscott, MA 01907
(617) 595-1556

OBJECTIVE: To continue my progressive and successful career in Purchasing.

QUALIFIED BY: Extensive and progressive senior-level purchasing experience for a major organization, highlighted by consistent cost-saving and efficiency-enhancing achievements.

Significant capabilities include: Vendor negotiations; troubleshooting around schedules; product quality; expediting; workflow coordination; procurement responsibility up to $2 million in multiple locations; computerized purchasing systems; needs assessment; staff supervision; multi-department management.

DIRECT EXPERIENCE: Bank of Boston   Boston, MA
Promoted through several positions of increasing responsibility, including:

Senior Buyer/Assistant Purchasing Officer
(1979–1989)
Managed the procurement of general bank supplies, including materials-handling equipment, check-processing equipment, security/protection equipment, numerous printed forms used both externally and internally, and paper products for all locations. Also served as sole procurement representative in the Bank's Canton facility, responsible for all purchasing requirements for 700+ staff (excepting furniture and contracts).

*Exemplary
Achievements:*

- Researched, developed, and instituted a corporation-wide contract for copy paper (130 million sheets). Negotiated firm pricing for nine months. *Result:* savings of $90,000 for 1990. (System still in place today.)

**OTHER
EXPERIENCE:**

Marblehead Marine Services Marblehead, MA Responsible Head Rigger position (1990–present) requires staff supervision, record keeping (time and supply use for billing), and rigging operations for approximately 800 boats per year.

Interact with a wide range of MMS customers, both commercial and pleasure boat owners and operators.

Other responsibilities have included: . . .

- In his Bank of Boston job section, John made the dates less prominent, moving them into the body of the résumé, downplaying the present nature of his employment situation.
- Finally, John made some style changes that worked to his advantage. He removed the bold style of his title Head Rigger and kept the bold for his title of Senior Buyer/Assistant Purchasing Officer.

Without altering any of his background data, John was able to design a new résumé to set a positive tone, greatly reduce negative perceptions, capitalize on his strengths, and focus his audience on his relevant and valuable assets in his desired professional specialty.

17. You Look Like a Job Hopper

Fortunately, short-term employment is not the stigma it used to be. A generation ago, it was not unusual for one's career to have consisted of one job with one company. Job hoppers were thought of as those "who couldn't hold down a job." Now statistics show a completely different work world. The average worker under the age of 35 changes jobs every year and a half. The average worker over the age of 35 changes jobs every three years. Clearly job hopping is more common than ever before.

So how do companies interpret this? Obviously they don't want high turnover, which results in higher costs, such as recruitment and retraining expenses. Certainly companies *want* the ideal employee, that is, one who is loyal, productive, and stimulating and who stays that way and with them, for a long time. They realize, however, that this can be unrealistic in this day and age. So they also look for value and depth of contribution with each job within each company, whether short or long term.

Astute companies know that valuable employees are often recruited from one company to the next because of their worth. In fact, it's often the companies themselves—and their appealing offers to valuable employees—that can make the valuable employee into a job hopper. So it is just as often worth as it is lack of worth that is the cause of short-term employment in today's market.

This is not to say, however, that you shouldn't downplay the fact that you moved around a lot. In most industries, companies have grown to accept two or three years with one company as acceptable. However, if you've had several one-year stints with companies, it's best to downplay the dates and build on your contributions within each company.

Take a look at job hopper John Barton's first résumé on the next page.

JOHN BARTON'S FIRST RÉSUMÉ

**PROFESSIONAL
EXPERIENCE:**

4/92–Present	Coastal Hills Company Erskin, OR **East Coast Sales Manager** Set up a sales and distribution network. Formulated programs and pricing. Worked with distribution salespeople in different markets. Opened new markets.
12/90–11/91	Western Wine & Spirits, Ltd. Costa Mesa, CA **Regional Sales Manager**—New England Directed sales and marketing of a portfolio of a wide variety of wine products. Motivated and co-directed a sales force of 15.
12/89–9/90	Wine Products, Ltd. Chicago, IL **Division Manager**—New England and Mid- Atlantic Division Directed strategic sales and distribution planning for new product development. Responsible for pricing and programming with distributors, coordinating market surveys, preparing monthly depletion reports. Conducted sales meetings and seminars. Maintained and developed key account relations. **District Manager**—New England
8/88–10/89	Eastern Wines & Spirits of Boston Boston, MA **Salesman**

JOHN BARTON'S NEW RÉSUMÉ

**PROFESSIONAL
EXPERIENCE:**

Coastal Hills Company   Erskin, OR
East Coast Sales Manager (1992–present)
To date, have set up a sales and distribution
network, formulated programs and pricing,
and worked effectively with distribution
salespeople in different markets.

Achievements:

- Opened five new markets within nine months.
- Placed Coastal's wine list at Walt Disney properties.
- Placed Coastal in State of Pennsylvania contracted stores.
- Placed Coastal as featured wine at major restaurants, including Pillar House and Parker House.
- Arranged for Coastal to be billed as one of ten participants in nationally known Southwest Florida Wine Festival.

Western Wine & Spirits, Ltd.   Costa Mesa, CA
Regional Sales Manager—New England
(1990–1991)
Directed sales and marketing of a portfolio of
a wide variety of wine products. Motivated
and co-directed a sales force of 15.

Achievements:

- Placed Oak Ridge Wine in the States of Connecticut and Rhode Island.
- Increased 1991 sales 3% over 1990.

Wine Products, Ltd.   Chicago, IL
Division Manager—New England and Mid-
Atlantic Division (1989–1990)
Directed strategic sales and distribution planning
for new product development. Responsible

for pricing and programming with distributors, coordinating market surveys, preparing monthly depletion reports. Conducted sales meetings and seminars. Maintained and developed key account relations.
District Manager—New England

Achievements: • 1989 sales increased 18.5%.

Eastern Wines & Spirits of Boston   Boston, MA
Salesman (1988–1989)

Achievements: • Increased sales over 60%.

It is clear that John's first résumé does not make him a hot date! A quick scan of the obvious left-margin dates tell us that John hasn't stuck around more than a year for any of his last four jobs. Further, it doesn't take an astute reader to see that John wasn't recruited to his next jobs; there's a clear gap between positions. Finally, there's no way for the reader to know whether John performed effectively in his positions, because he didn't list any achievements.

Yet John *was* a good performer. Indeed, it was circumstances outside of his performance—a company takeover, a forced relocation requirement, a difficult and irrational senior Vice President whom no one could get along with—that forced his job changes. John didn't deserve the negative attention his résumé gave him. And his rewrite helped him enormously. See John's new résumé on page 70.

In John's new résumé, he has moved the dates inside the body of the résumé, taking the attention away from them. Most importantly, he has removed the months, listing only the years of his employment. This is still accurate and ethical. He hasn't falsified a thing. The result of using just years and not months has helped in two ways: John's jobs now appear to have the potential of having lasted up to two years each rather than less than one. Further, it now appears possible that John could have been recruited directly into each new position, rather than, as the months would indicate, being stuck with gaps in his employment history. Finally, John gave some thought to what he accomplished in each position and then listed this on the résumé. In addition to beefing up his value, John was able to focus the reader away from the dates and onto his achievements.

Since a résumé is objective fact it can't be subjective or make excuses. The time for that is at the interview. In John's case, his objective data in his first résumé was hurting him, depriving him of the opportunity to explain his job changes. His second résumé ethically and persuasively manipulates the data to give him the opportunity he needs.

18. It Appears That You Stayed Too Long with One Company

Believe it or not, staying too long with one employer in this day and age can be construed as a negative as often as it is a positive. One position with one company for 10 years, for example, can make you appear to be an unambitious slider, unmotivated to grow. That may be an injustice and you actually may have been ideally matched to your position, but you need to show that on your résumé; otherwise the reader may not see an exciting contributor on paper. If you've spent more than five years in one position with one company, be sure to show your growth and contributions in that position. Don't look stagnant. For an example, see the following résumé:

**PROFESSIONAL
EXPERIENCE:**
1978–Present

Johnson & Silkwood, C.P.A.'s Dartmouth, NH
A busy C.P.A. firm with six professionals and
two support staff providing a diverse range
of client services, including all aspects of
accounting work and management advisory
services.

C.P.A. and Firm Manager
Consistently absorb increasing levels of
responsibility within this position.

- Work directly with corporate, partnership, and
  individual clients in areas of reviews,
  audits, compilations, taxes, and forecasts.
  Provide financing and acquisition advice,
  in addition to assistance in the set-up of
  computerized accounting and bookkeeping
  systems.

- Concurrently serve as firm's manager,
  maintaining management authority over
  other professionals and support staff. Handle
  supervision, scheduling, some hiring and
  performance review, work review (including
  partners). Assist in time billing processes;
  make billing judgments; serve as health plan
  administrator.

- Play an active role in the firm's promotion
  and image, representing the firm in visible
  and productive community activities.

If you've had several jobs with one employer, show this as progressive experience. Don't repeat the company name each time. Instead, place the overall time of company employment in the left margin across from the company name, and list your specific positions in reverse chronological order with the dates of that position after each title. See below for what John Jones, a purchasing professional from the Bank of Boston, did.

JOHN JONES' RÉSUMÉ

EXPERIENCE:

1969–1992   Bank of Boston   Boston, MA
Promoted through several positions of increasing responsibility, including:

1989–1992   **Senior Buyer/Assistant Purchasing Officer**
Managed the procurement of general bank supplies, including materials-handling equipment, check-processing equipment, security/protection equipment, numerous printed forms used both externally and internally, and paper products for all locations. Also served as sole procurement representative in the Bank's Canton facility, responsible for all purchasing requirements for 700+ staff.

Exemplary Achievements:

• Researched, developed, and instituted a corporation-wide contract for copy paper (130 million sheets). Negotiated firm pricing for nine months. *Result:* savings of $90,000 for 1990. (System still in place today).

• Completed an extensive listing of non-printed inventory, went out to bid for and obtained one comprehensive vendor. *Result:* reduced purchase order time, buyer time, inventory space and stock-outs. (Before this system, average processing cost of *each purchase* order had reached $75! New system still in place today.)

- Developed and instituted a low-volume contract for certain stock inventory items. *Result:* one vendor, one purchase order (300+ items), and no inventory retained in Supply Department. (System still in place today.)

1979–1989

Manager, Duplication and Addressograph Departments
Managed daily operations of both departments, coordinated jobs, developed and managed budgets for corresponding departments, managed staff of 18 support and supervisory personnel.
- Designed a method for printing proxy cards that resulted in accelerated turnaround and improved productivity.

Supervisor, Duplication Dept. (1975–1979)

Support Staff (1969–75)

Always try to play devil's advocate regarding how your background might look on paper. Don't assume the reader will understand your situation. Remember, other than what is on your résumé, your reader usually knows nothing about you. Your job history on paper is wide open to interpretation. Help the reader to draw the right conclusions.

19. Your Current Job Title Looks Like a Step Backward

Ms. Palmer, the Assistant Controller at The Kernsworth Company, had long aspired to a full Controller position. That opportunity actually came with her own employer when the firm's Controller became seriously ill and was forced to retire early. Palmer was given the responsibilities of the Controller position on a temporary basis during the company's thorough search for the old Controller's replacement. And Palmer did a good job. In fact, she did everything that was expected of her. But after the company's search was completed, she was notified that she came in second for the job (it was given to a Kernsworth Controller from another division); she would be returning to her old position of Assistant Controller.

This did not sit well with Palmer, and she resumed her own outside search for a Controller position. When she went to develop her résumé, she was optimistic because she felt she could finally put down experience at the Controller, rather than Assistant Controller, level. But she soon realized that one thing stuck out like a sore thumb: She had gone up from Assistant Controller to Controller and back down to Assistant Controller. The results of her first résumé depressed her. See what the critical part of her first résumé looked like on the next page.

MS. PALMER'S FIRST RÉSUMÉ

OBJECTIVE: Corporate Controller, Domestic or International.

**PROFESSIONAL
EXPERIENCE:**
1981–Present   The Kernsworth Company   Marshfield, MA

Assistant Controller (4/91–present)
Primary responsibility for assisting the Division's
Controller in all aspects of financial
operations of 15 international subsidiaries.
Coordinated accounting, budgeting, and
strategic planning process, as well as tax/treasury
functions.

Controller (11/90–4/91)
Over a nine-month period, took over Controller's
position and directed the financial operations
of all international subsidiaries located in the
Far East, Europe, Latin America, and
Canada.

Assistant Controller (7/90–11/90)
Primary responsibility for assisting the Division's
Controller in all aspects of financial
operations of 15 international subsidiaries.
Coordinated accounting, budgeting, and
strategic planning process, as well as tax/treasury
functions.

Director of Accounting and Budgets—
International Division (5/89–7/90)
Responsible for subsidiaries' financials and export
subsidiary accounting. Directed consolidation
of monthly estimates, annual budget, and
strategic plans.

Manager, Financial Planning and Budgets—
International Division (5/87–5/89)
Prepared acquisition financial analyses.
Coordinated the consolidation and reporting
of operating budgets, strategic plans, and
estimates.

Budget Analyst—International Division
(5/86–5/87)
Coordinated the consolidation, analyses, and
reporting of financial data from international
subsidiaries for monthly actuals, estimates,
annual budget, and latest estimate
presentation to general management.

Senior Tax Accountant (10/81–5/86)
Responsible for state taxes, DISC, FSC, and
analysis of monthly income tax provision.
Worked with parent company tax department
for filing income taxes.

Palmer knew she needed to communicate her effectiveness
during her stint as Controller, as well as explain to the reader why
she went back to her old job of Assistant Controller. The more she
thought about it, the more she realized that what happened to her
was logical and all she needed to do was guide the reader through an
explanation. She knew she could explain the situation in her cover
letter, but she was afraid that relying on the cover letter alone to
cover this critical area of information would be risky, since the
résumé could get separated from the cover letter or the cover letter
might not get read. So she went about building a new résumé (see
the next page) that put her in the best possible light.

MS. PALMER'S NEW RÉSUMÉ

OBJECTIVE: Corporate Controller, Domestic/International.

QUALIFIED BY: Twelve years of experience in corporate finance, advancing through five major positions of increasing responsibility. Highlights include:
- effectively serving as Interim Controller and Assistant Controller
- eight years in tax-related work; knowledge of foreign tax codes
- six years in international finance and accounting
- experience in financial analysis of acquisitions and divestments
- coordinating accounting, budgeting, strategic planning, tax/treasury, and office automation functions.

PROFESSIONAL EXPERIENCE:

1981–Present   The Kernsworth Company   Marshfield, MA

Interim Controller (1990–1991)/**Assistant Controller** (1990–present)
As Interim Controller, International Division, responsibilities over a nine-month period included directing the financial operations of 15 international subsidiaries located in the Far East, Europe, Latin America, and Canada. Coordinated accounting, budgeting and strategic planning process, as well as tax/treasury functions.
- Developed a realistic budgeting mentality that set attainable goals in place of previously unreachable goals, and has resulted in higher morale and sense of accomplishment. (In 1991 we exceeded budget by $3 million.)

- Received excellent performance reviews for accomplishing all objectives as Interim Controller; smoothly facilitated transition for new Controller (a senior ranking Controller from another Kernsworth location).

Director of Accounting and Budgets—
International Division (5/89–7/90)
Responsible for subsidiaries' financials and export subsidiary accounting. Directed consolidation of monthly estimates, annual budget, and strategic plans.

Manager, Financial Planning and Budgets—
International Division (5/87–5/89)
Prepared acquisition financial analyses. Coordinated the consolidation and reporting of operating budgets, strategic plans, and estimates.

Budget Analyst—International Division (5/86–5/87)
Coordinated the consolidation, analyses, and reporting of financial data from international subsidiaries for monthly actuals, estimates, annual budget, and latest estimate presentation to general management.

Senior Tax Accountant (10/81–5/86)

Notice the summary Palmer built in under the category Qualified By. In this early section she introduces the title Interim Controller. This title sets the tone for the reader, showing the temporary nature of the position from the very beginning, so the reader is not surprised by her return to Assistant Controller. Further, the summary section qualifies her performance, setting a positive tone by stating that she "effectively" served as Interim Controller and Assistant Controller. Then, in describing her positions in The Kernsworth Company, she lists Interim Controller first and describes her responsibilities and achievements within that position. Despite the fact that her current position is Assistant Controller, she has logically listed her highest level of responsibility first: Interim Controller. Then she goes on to show her effectiveness in the position: "Received excellent performance reviews for accomplishing all objectives as Interim Controller..." Finally, she even gets in the reason for her not being selected as permanent Controller: "Smoothly facilitated transition for new Controller (a senior ranking Controller from another Kernsworth location)."

Palmer felt confident that, on paper, she'd put herself in the best possible light, proving that, though she was currently titled Assistant Controller, she could successfully handle the full responsibilities of the Controller position.

20. Your Résumé Sounds Stuck in the Past Tense

Don't feel you have to write in the past tense. Past tense sounds like a "has-been." Instead use the present participle (the "ing" form). This will give your résumé a much more active sound. Vicki Marston's first résumé (see page 82), for example, sounded stale and inactive. She'd lost her job when the airline she worked for went under. Now on paper her career looked stuck in the past tense.

VICKI'S FIRST RÉSUMÉ

**RELEVANT
EXPERIENCE:**
1988–1991   Bass Harbor Airlines   Boston, MA

Sales Coordinator
Acted as liaison between outside sales
representative and travel agent/client.
Participated in promotional activities and trade
shows. Coordinated and hosted familiarization
trips. Maintained knowledge of data base.
Prepared contracts and sale closures.

Sales Service Agent
Applied in-depth knowledge of international
ticket sales. Generated weekly sales reports.
Assisted with group sales. Worked directly with
sales representatives and travel agencies.
Utilized proficiency with SCORE computer
systems.

Vicki developed a new résumé (see next page) that was much more active. She moved the dates away from the prominent left margin to downplay the past tense. Then she broke up the paragraph format into bullets, which accentuated the more active verb form she used to begin each line.

VICKI'S NEW RÉSUMÉ

**RELEVANT
EXPERIENCE:**   Bass Harbor Airlines   Boston, MA

Sales Coordinator (1990–1991)
Promoted to this position with responsibilities that included:

- acting as liaison between outside sales and travel agent/client
- participating in promotional activities and trade shows
- coordinating and hosting familiarization trips
- maintaining knowledge of data base
- preparing contracts and sale closures

Sales Service Agent (1988–1990)
Entrusted with key responsibilities that included:

- applying in-depth knowledge of international ticket sales
- generating weekly sales reports
- assisting with group sales
- working directly with sales representatives and travel agencies
- utilizing proficiency with SCORE computer systems

---

21. Your Career Spans So Many Years You Feel You Have Too Much Past

There is no rule that says how many years you need to include in your résumé. The résumé's only goal is to be persuasive. Regardless of your reasons for job changes, showing a long string of jobs on your résumé is counterproductive to the goal of being persuasive. The reader's first reaction is: "Gee, this person's had *lots* of jobs." Concentrate on your most recent relevant experience. Make that information as detailed as possible. Showing the 1960s on your résumé will do you no good; that was two and a half decades ago. Even the 1970s may not be timely enough. That experience, whether technical or managerial, is most likely irrelevant. What you learned then, the people you knew, and how you did things—all have probably changed significantly.

And what if your early career experience has some merit but still looks like a long string of jobs? This is what Helen Arvis encountered when she prepared her résumé for another health-care marketing position. She knew her background as a nurse was a good foundation, but she'd been a staff nurse for 16 years at five different hospitals. She felt listing each job in a detailed format on her résumé would waste valuable space and make her early career look unstable. In fact, she couldn't keep her résumé to one page and do justice to her most relevant experience if she listed all her professional health-care experience since college. See what Helen's first résumé looked like on the next page.

Helen was disappointed when she finished her first résumé, for two reasons: There wasn't room to develop a summary or expand her marketing experience, and it was clear at first glance that she'd had a page-full of different employers.

Helen found the solution by summarizing her 16 years of nursing under a Nursing Background category, with the dates moved out of the left margin to inside the body of the résumé. This three-line summary conveyed enough information to show the reader she had a solid nursing foundation, and, more importantly, it freed up 14 lines for more important data. It allowed her space to develop a Qualified

HELEN'S FIRST RÉSUMÉ

HELEN B. ARVIS
126 Oakwood Lane
Swampscott, MA 01907
(617) 563-1899

OBJECTIVE: Sales/Marketing position within the health-care industry.

EXPERIENCE:

1991–Present

Medical Services, Inc.   Concord, NH
Marketing Representative
— Broad-based responsibilities with primary role in the marketing of the Center's MRI program to physicians, including neurosurgeons, neurologists, orthopedic surgeons, and other specialists.

1988–1990

New Medico Associates   Lynn, MA
Corporate-Based Marketer
— Promoted products and services of national health-care company to physicians, health-care providers, families, and funding sources.
— Called on and maintained existing contacts; developed major prospects.
— Identified current trends and needs of prospects to assist public relations department in developing mass and trade media pieces.

1987–1988

Boston City Hospital   Boston, MA
Staff Nurse
— Handled all aspects of patient care for the medical-surgical floor of this major city hospital.

1987	**Salem Hospital**	Salem, MA

Staff Nurse
- Served on a pediatric nursing floor. Extensive patient teaching responsibilities. Rotated as Charge Nurse.

1981–1987   Massachusetts General Hospital   Boston, MA
Staff Nurse
- Handled all aspects of patient care on a medical-surgical floor.

1977–1981   Beverly Hospital   Beverly, MA
Staff Nurse
- Provided patient care on a pediatric nursing floor of this 125-bed suburban hospital.

1972–1977   Lawrence General Hospital   Lawrence, MA
Staff Nurse—medical-surgical floor

EDUCATION: Westfield State College, Westfield, MA
Bachelor of Science in Business, 1989. Minor in Management.

Salem State College, Salem, MA
Diploma in Nursing, 1972.

REFERENCES: Provided upon request.

By section, an enlarged description section under her two most important jobs, and an Achievements section under her current and most valuable position. Additionally, at first glance, her new résumé appeared to show her as having had just two jobs (not seven), both of which were focused in the area of her career objective. Here is what Helen's new résumé looked like:

HELEN'S NEW RÉSUMÉ

HELEN B. ARVIS
126 Oakwood Lane
Swampscott, MA 01907
(617) 563-1899

OBJECTIVE: Sales/Marketing position within the health-care industry.

QUALIFIED BY: Six-year professional background in health-care sales, marketing, and direct-care services. Significant capabilities include:

- new market development, direct sales and account management
- market research, trend identification and analysis, sales tracking
- public and media relations, development of marketing materials.

HEALTH CARE MARKETING EXPERIENCE:

1991–Present

Medical Services, Inc.   Concord, NH
A consortium of six community hospitals that sponsors two programs: the Center for Radiation Oncology and the Center for MRI
Marketing Representative
- Broad-based responsibilities with primary role in the marketing of the Center's MRI program to physicians, including neurosurgeons, neurologists, orthopedic surgeons, and other specialists.
- Additionally handled all public relations, including press releases to community newspapers, hospital medical staff letters.
- Coordinated/hosted open house parties for referring physician offices.

- Designed all marketing materials; coordinated Physician Education Speaker Programs; prepared/presented MRI exhibit to sponsoring hospitals.
- Produced two cable television magazine format programs (30 min.).
- Developed marketing base to track referrals and coordinate market data.

Achievements:
- Increased MRI physician referral base by 121%, resulting in a maximum volume of MRI scans each month.

1988–1990   New Medico Associates   Lynn, MA
Corporate-Based Marketer
- Promoted products and services of national health-care company to physicians, health care providers, families, and funding sources.
- Called on and maintained existing contacts; developed major prospects.
- Identified current trends and needs of prospects to assist public relations department in developing mass and trade media pieces.

**NURSING
BACKGROUND:**   Between 1972 and 1988 gained a valuable foundation in the health-care industry as a Staff Nurse for several major hospitals in the Boston area. Details upon request.

EDUCATION: Westfield State College, Westfield, MA
Bachelor of Science in Business, 1989. Minor in Management.

Salem State College, Salem, MA
Diploma in Nursing, 1972.

REFERENCES: Provided from above employers and others upon request.

22. You Look Inexperienced or Underqualified

Begin by asking yourself these questions: Why do I know I can do the job? Why does what little experience I have prove to me that this is where I want to and should be? Even if I don't have the best training, skills, or experience, why is my ability and/or aptitude right for the position? What kind of person does it take to thrive in the position? What is easily trainable and moldable about me?

Ask others about the type of position or industry you're interested in. Find out what raw materials the position or industry typically utilizes in its people. Ask around. Be a sleuth.

When you find these answers, write a Profile at the top of your résumé that outlines these valuable qualities of yours. This will set the right tone for your readers, showing your audience that you've done your homework and know what kind of person is right for their particular position or industry. Furthermore, you'll be showing that you know yourself and feel you're a good match for them.

After you set the tone through the Profile section, study what you've written. Think about what you know as it relates to the kind of position or industry to which you're headed. Ask yourself: What parts of my background would reinforce the Profile I've written? How can I delineate my job or educational experience in such a way that the readers of my résumé can see the value of such experience in their business or industry?

When Howard Willisburn built his first résumé (see page 90) after college, he looked at it and yawned. He knew he wanted to get into the fitness field at a management level, and he knew he'd be very effective at it. But his first résumé didn't come close to conveying that.

HOWARD'S FIRST RÉSUMÉ

HOWARD A. WILLISBURN
47 Elgin Street
Hingham, MA 02043
(617) 749-5589

OBJECTIVE: A responsible position in the health/fitness field.

EDUCATION: Salem State College   Salem, MA
Bachelor of Arts Degree, English, 5/92
• Concentration: Fitness
• Intern: GTE Corporation Fitness Center
  (9/90–12/90)

Quaboag Regional High School   Warren, MA
Graduate, 1988

EMPLOYMENT EXPERIENCE:

1991–Present   Pyramid Books   Salem, MA

Clerk
• Responsible position requiring working
  independently, customer relations, order
  processing into computer, opening and closing,
  and direct sales.

1989–1991   Crosby's Market   Salem, MA

Cashier/Deli
• Responsible for full operation of electronic cash
  register systems.
• Additionally, served in a customer service
  capacity at Crosby's busy deli counter.

1989–1990   Yankee Spirits   Sturbridge, MA
(summers)

Cashier/Deli
Similar responsibilities to those at above position.

1983–1988 (summers)	Howard's Drive-in	West Brookfield, MA

Counter/Short Order Cook, Scheduler
Responsible for a several positions in this busy drive-in.

INTERESTS: Numerous outdoor sports.

REFERENCES: Provided upon request.

Before he rebuilt his résumé, Howard did something smart: He made a list of the points he wanted to get across. He answered his own question: Why do I know I'd make a good manager in the fitness field?

His answers were:

Because I know how to work with all types of people, I have the right attitude, and I know this is critical to generate new business and happy clients in the fitness service industry.
Because I've actually interned in a fitness center learning all facets of its operations, and therefore I'm sure I'm comfortable in that type of environment.
Because I've studied fitness, diet, and exercise, along with fitness management.
Because I "practice what I preach"; this shows in my active lifestyle and my own personal diet and fitness concerns.
Because I'm not afraid of hard work; I worked throughout my college years.
Because I can manage as well as teach; I was appointed Assistant Teacher to the Swim Class Coach in college.

From this outline Howard wrote his profile and strengthened his résumé. See what Howard's new résumé looked like when completed on pages 92 and 93.

HOWARD'S NEW RÉSUMÉ

HOWARD A. WILLISBURN
47 Elgin Street
Hingham, MA 02043
(617) 749-5589

OBJECTIVE: Responsible position in the health/fitness field that could benefit from my relevant education, consistent fitness career interest, and practical experience.

PROFILE:
- Conscientious employee with a strong work ethic, a positive attitude, and consistent commitment to customers'/clients' needs.
- Bachelor's Degree with a minor in Sports, Fitness and Leisure.
- Corporate field study in a major company's fitness center.
- Consistent interest and belief in proper diet and fitness.
- Comfortable in both a teaching and management role.
- Active outdoor lifestyle.

EDUCATION: Salem State College   Salem, MA
Bachelor of Arts Degree, with Fitness Minor, 5/92

- Specialized coursework included: Diet and Exercise, Senior Citizens Fitness, Fitness Management, Aquatics.
- Appointed as Assistant Teacher to Swim Class Coach; worked with small groups on various strokes and breathing methods.

Quaboag Regional High School   Warren, MA
Graduate, 1988

- Active tennis player
- Honor role (twice)

**FIELD
EXPERIENCE:**   GTE Corporation

Field Study—GTE Fitness Center (1990)

- Learned all aspects of fitness center operations, including computer system, record keeping, equipment types and operation, scheduling and customer (employee) services.

- Handled fitness testing, set up machine schedules for users, instructed on selection and use of proper toning machines, ensured that users were relaxed and comfortable in the facility and on the equipment.

**CUSTOMER
SERVICE
EXPERIENCE:**   Pyramid Books, Salem, MA (6/91–present)
Crosby's Market, Salem, MA (during school year, 1989–1991)
Yankee Spirits, Sturbridge, MA (summers, 1989–1990)
Howard's Drive-in, W. Brookfield, MA (summers, 1983–1988)

CERTIFICATES: Lifeguard Certificate (in process of renewal)
CPR (in process of renewal)

INTERESTS: Boating (sailing, water skiing), swimming, running, hiking, travel.

REFERENCES: Provided from above employers and GTE Fitness Center upon request.

Let's look at what he did.

First, Howard's new objective brings the word "benefit" into the text, appropriately focusing on his value as matched to the reader's needs.

Howard's new Profile section has set the right tone for the reader, incorporating the key points from his outline.

His education section has now highlighted his Fitness minor rather than his English major. Further, he has elaborated on his fitness-related coursework to show technical, teaching, and management exposure. He has shown his activity in sports and achievements in academics in high school.

He has detailed his critical field study experience at GTE Fitness Center, placing this in the middle of the résumé, where it will get attention. He also has taken the months out and used just the calendar year of 1990.

Instead of labeling the next category Employment Experience, Howard has emphasized what he knows to be valuable customer service experience by labeling the category as such. This gets the reader to think of Howard's college job as valuable customer interaction rather than just part-time hourly positions necessary to pay the bills during school. He knows that the titles of his positions or their descriptions will do him no good and take up valuable space. His old résumé made him look like a clerk and cashier; he was glad to get away from that appearance.

In Howard's old résumé, he hadn't listed what he knew were two valuable certifications because they had both expired. When building his new résumé, he realized that renewing them was not a problem and would not take long. So he further strengthened his résumé by adding the Certificates category.

Howard strengthened his Interests section to give a picture of his athletic abilities.

Finally, he empowered his References category by, in effect, telling the reader that his field-study performance at GTE Fitness Center was successful.

23. You Want to Change Careers but Don't Have the Right Professional Background

Sharon Burns had this type of problem. Professionally she'd been a Controller and Office Manager for a small manufacturer for more than 12 years. But that had been her income, not her life, and she was not happy in her job. Her real love was development (fund-raising). Over the years she had enjoyed and been successful at planning, organizing, and implementing fund-raising activities for various non-profits such as her church, her son's school, and small charitable organizations. Now she wanted to get paid for what she did so well. When she first wrote her résumé (see page 96) she wasn't happy with the results.

Sharon knew she had to guide the reader away from her career as a Controller and Office Manager. She also knew she had to convince her reader that she was very capable in development and could do professionally what she had done as a volunteer. She needed to change the tone of the whole résumé to be one focused on development.

First she wrote a development-focused objective that alluded to the value of both her business and development experience. Then she wrote a summary that concentrated on development. After this she led the reader directly into her development background. In the section entitled Development Experience, she qualified and quantified her achievements in development, highlighting them in bullet form in a prominent spot (the middle) of the résumé. Finally, at the end of the résumé she listed her less-relevant employment with Water Cooling Company. See how development professional Sharon Burns' new résumé looked like on page 98.

SHARON'S FIRST RÉSUMÉ

SHARON BURNS
38 East Shore Drive
Nahant, MA 01923
(617) 526-6370

OBJECTIVE: Professional position in Development.

**WORK
EXPERIENCE:**

1979–Present   Water Cooling Company, Inc.   Nahant, MA
A manufacturer and distributor of industrial
cooling equipment.

Controller and Office Manager
Responsible for administrative, credit, and
customer service functions for this small
manufacturer and distributor of cooling
equipment.

Extensive and diverse business experience in
the administration, credit, and customer
service functions.

Responsibilities include:
- handling credit functions and accounts
  receivable
- interacting with vendors and customers
- serving as liaison between management and
  production personnel
- meeting materials planning needs
- working under pressure to meet deadlines
- managing catalog production, including copy,
  ad agency, printer, and mail house liaison
- setting up booths and selling at trade shows

EDUCATION: Salem State College, **Ed.M.**
Wheaton College, **B.A., Economics**
London School of Economics, junior year abroad

John Brown Seminar in **Planned Giving and Fund-raising for Charitable Institutions**, Certificate

**VOLUNTEER
EXPERIENCE:**   **Chair for the Capital Fund Drive of the Unitarian Universalist Church of Marblehead, MA** (1987–1990).

Fund-raising Chairperson for the Boston Youth-At-Risk Program (1986).

Regional Chair for Northfield-Mount Hermon School Capital Fund (1985–1986).

REFERENCES: Provided upon request.

SHARON'S NEW RÉSUMÉ

SHARON BURNS
38 East Shore Drive
Nahant, MA 01923
(617) 526-6370

OBJECTIVE: Position in Development utilizing strong background in business management and in directing capital fund-raising campaigns.

SUMMARY: Extensive and diverse experience in the planning, design, and implementation of successful fund-raising activities for educational, fine arts, and religious institutions, and community programs. Specific expertise includes:
- Leading annual fund-raising drives and capital campaigns for organizations that have attained highest levels of giving and participation nationwide.
- Developing and marketing overall fund-raising plans and strategies.
- Recruiting and training volunteers from diverse groups.
- Qualifying and targeting potential contributors.
- Organizing and managing calling campaigns, annual telethons.
- Planning logistics for fund-raising events: site selection, program development, solicitation of donated items.
- Creating and designing high-impact letters and mission statements.

DEVELOPMENT EXPERIENCE: **As Chair for the Capital Fund Drive of the Unitarian Universalist Church of Marblehead, MA** (1987–1990):
- Managed three-year Capital Fund Drive that generated the highest levels of giving in the church's 275-year history.

- Created financial reporting systems for tracking of donations; established required accounts at financial institutions to meet campaign requirements.
- Trained and tracked volunteers in solicitation methods, set up feedback mechanism to insure proper coverage and reporting of results.

As Fund-raising Chairperson for the Boston Youth-At-Risk Program (1986):
- Designed and conducted a compelling, year-long campaign for Youth-At-Risk that generated $280,000 in funds to support course for inner-city youth to teach self-responsibility and commitment to positive action.
- Integrated an effective volunteer core from diverse group of multi-ethnic, multi-racial, and broad socioeconomic backgrounds by tapping focused interests and building shared commitment toward common goal.

As Regional Chair for Northfield-Mount Hermon School Capital Fund (1985–1986):
- Chaired Capital Fund that resulted in the highest per capita donations and level of participation nationwide.

EDUCATION: Salem State College, **Ed.M.**
Wheaton College, **B.A., Economics**
John Brown Seminar in **Planned Giving and Fund-raising for Charitable Institutions**, Certificate

BUSINESS EXPERIENCE: Water Cooling Company, Inc.   Nahant, MA
Controller/Office Manager
Responsible for administrative, credit, and customer-service functions for this manufacturer and distributor of cooling equipment (1979–present).

24. Your Education Is Your Weakness

If your education is not your strong point you obviously don't want it in a prominent position in your résumé. In fact, there is no rule that says you must list your education at all on your résumé if you don't feel it's relevant. If your education is clearly too limited for the level of position you seek, try to build up your practical experience as much as possible. Draw the reader into your work experience, absorbing his attention in that area. Concentrate on achievements or specific projects that highlight your valuable real-world experience. If you do a good job, the reader may never notice your lack of education. Or the reader may say to himself: "Well, I don't see a degree here, but he sure has valuable on-the-job background."

If you've received specialized training, attended industry seminars, or received certificates, you might want to put this under a category called Professional Development or Specialized Training. By avoiding the category Education, you don't remind the reader to look for formal education, but instead keep him focused on your specialized background.

When Peter Bartlett wanted to switch firms in his field of construction management, he knew he was up against professionals with bachelor's degrees and even some M.B.A.s. He didn't want to draw attention to his education, so he concentrated on his direct field experience, drawing the reader's attention toward his specific projects to exemplify his abilities. See Peter's résumé on the next page.

PETER'S RÉSUMÉ

PETER J. BARTLETT
44 Stollson Street
Minneapolis, MN 55405
(612) 745-6632

OBJECTIVE: Senior Level Construction Management—
Industrial and Process

QUALIFIED BY: More than 15 years of progressive industry
experience specializing in industrial
wastewater treatment/industrial process-related
construction.
Strengths include:
* Managing multiple field, multi-system projects;
  directing field staff.
* Consistently meeting time milestones and
  budget targets on fixed-fee projects in even
  the most difficult, multiple-change order
  environments.

EXPERIENCE:
1988–Present

McKeon Corporation   Minneapolis, MN
A civil and mechanical construction general
contractor performing industrial and
wastewater treatment projects.

Progressed through positions of increasing
responsibility, including:
Apprentice, Journeyman, Foreman, General
Foreman, Superintendent, Project Manager,
Contract Manager, and Vice President (current).

Vice President
Responsible for overall project organization,
planning, on-site management, and direction
of project teams and their activities.

Project Experience:
- *Advanced Wastewater Treatment Facility*, Webster-Dudley, MA: $35 million secondary and advanced treatment facilities to existing plant.
- *Coal-Fired Heat Plant*, Malmstrom AFB, Great Falls, MT: $35 million new coal-fired, high-pressure, hot-water generator, central plant, and distribution system, including installation of 75,000 feet of outside distribution connecting to 68 facilities requiring conversion to a high-temperature hot-water system.
- *Trident II Submarine Training Facility*, St. Mary's, GA: $25 million, 550,000 SF training facility with successful completion within 160-day deadline.
- *Carver-Greenfield Sludge Dehydration Facility, Sludge Control and Belt Conveyor Facility*, Carson, CA: $56 million prototype facility project requiring complex scheduling requirements, piping, and multi-system, multi-facility construction, including a 123,000 SF structure.
- *Regional Wastewater Treatment Facility*, Henrico, VA: $45 million, 30 MGD wastewater treatment plant with 42 structures, including oxygen and ozone generation facilities.

1981–1988   Oxford Industrial Building   Oxford, MA
A small commercial/industrial construction firm.

Foreman
Directed a wide range of projects between $3 million and $22 million.
- Gained a solid foundation in both construction and management operations, directing crew of 25 and handling project administration.
- Promoted from laborer to assistant foreman to foreman.

REFERENCES: Provided from above employers and others upon request.

Notice how Peter's résumé draws the reader into his project experience in detail, thereby placing the focus and the value on his direct experience. It doesn't even have an Education section. His earlier version did, and the last part looked like this:

1981–1988   Oxford Industrial Building   Oxford, MA
A small commercial/industrial construction firm.

Foreman
Directed a wide range of projects between $3 million and $22 million.
- Gained a solid foundation in both construction and management operations, directing crew of 25 and handling project administration.
- Promoted from laborer to assistant foreman to foreman.

EDUCATION:
1980   Abbot Community College   Beverly, MA
One year's study—liberal arts

1976–1980   Marblehead High School   Marblehead, MA
Graduate

REFERENCES: Provided from above employers and others upon request.

In this earlier version Peter's readers had no choice but to learn he had only one year of college. But in the résumé he successfully used, he didn't have to deal with that question until he got into the interview, and at that point he and the interviewer were well into a productive, harmonious meeting. After meeting with Peter, the interviewer decided Peter's lack of education was more than compensated for by his professional track record and ability to think on his feet.

25. You Work or Worked for a Company with a Poor or Bad Reputation

Don't accept guilt by association unless you have to. At times your employer's negative reputation may be completely out of your control, and it would be a shame to lose an interview opportunity because of an employer's bad name.

There are three possible ways to get around this, at least on paper:

- If the company has a parent corporation, it may be possible to use that name on your résumé. Many companies function under one dba (doing business as) which is well known to the public, but the actual paychecks come from a parent company with an unknown (untarnished) name. Technically, that parent company is the employer. Getting the reader to focus on your job within an organization rather than your association with an unsavory employer will give your résumé a better chance to communicate its message.
- If your company also sometimes refers to itself by its initials and the initials are less recognizable, using initials may be an option.
- If your job titles have as much or more value than the names of the companies for which you've worked, try visually highlighting your titles rather than the names of your employers. This will encourage the reader to concentrate on what you are, rather than where you are or were.
- If you can rearrange the order of your employer listings without jeopardizing the integrity of your résumé, you may want to do so. Perhaps by labeling another job as Primary Experience you can move the employer with the bad reputation to a less-obvious place.

26. Your Title Is More Impressive Than Your Company, or Vice Versa

Simply apply this formula: If your title is more impressive and persuasive to the reader, lead with the title in bold capital letters. Put your company on the next line under your job title in plain letters without any stylistic emphasis. *Example:*

EXPERIENCE:
1990–1992   **Branch Manager**
                   Frank's Sub Shop, Rochester, NY

In the opposite case, when your company is more impressive than your job title, lead with the company in bold capital letters and put your job title on the next line under it in plain letters. *Example:*

EXPERIENCE:
1990–1992   **International Business Machines Corporation**
                   Clerk Level III—Mail Room

---

27. A Company You Worked for or a School You Attended Is Not a Name Likely to Be Recognized by Your Reader

When this is the situation you want to build a case for the unknown place. If you know your company or school is a quality organization, ask yourself why that is so. Then qualify it the way you would qualify yourself. Educate the reader. What does the company or school have to be proud of? If you were writing a one-line descriptive marketing blurb about the organization, what would you say?

When George Metcalf's wife's job was moved from Boston to Cleveland, George knew he'd have to dust off his résumé and seek another job in his industry in Ohio. When he developed his résumé, the part about the job he was leaving behind looked like this:

EXPERIENCE:
1989–Present   Suburban Copier Repair Services   Marlboro, MA
                           Lead Technician

                           Responsible for servicing both commercial and office field accounts.
                           Troubleshoot and repair a wide range of copier types and brands...

George got little response from his résumé. It wasn't until he showed it to a friend at Suburban that he realized what he was doing wrong: He was not qualifying his company. No one in Ohio had heard of his company. More importantly, no one had any way of knowing how good a firm it was. Was it a mom-and-pop or a professional firm serving high-level industries and corporations?

George went back to the drawing board. Here's what he came up with:

EXPERIENCE:
1989–Present   **Lead Technician**

Suburban Copier Repair Services   Marlboro, MA

One of the area's leading copier repair services, with such major corporate accounts as Digital Equipment Corporation, Polaroid, Massachusetts General Hospital, and Harvard University.
In 1991 Suburban was rated "Service Company of the Year" by *Copy Magazine*.

Promoted to Lead Technician from among a highly trained and qualified staff of forty technicians servicing a total of 855 accounts...

George's new résumé downplays the name of his employer (since that name will mean nothing in Ohio) and highlights his title, which is much more important. Then it qualifies his company for the reader by listing Suburban's accounts and industry recognition. Suburban is obviously no mom-and-pop operation. George's new résumé actually educates the reader to realize that advancing to Lead Technician at Suburban must be quite an accomplishment. What company would entrust anyone other than a highly competent technician with such valuable and major corporate accounts? Furthermore, George mentions Suburban's award, demonstrating that he is a Lead Technician who is proud of what his company has achieved. Finally, he shows progressive experience, saying he was promoted from among a staff of 40 technicians. All in all, he now appears to be an attractive package!

28. You Are Looking for an Out-of-State Job

George Metcalf (see Winning Move #27) made one mistake he didn't know about when he sent his new, improved résumé from Boston to the Cleveland area. This mistake was the primary cause of his lack of response. The people in Cleveland saw this when they opened George's résumé:

GEORGE METCALF
18 Willow Road
Boston, MA 02115
(617) 532-8966

EXPERIENCE:
1989–Present   **Lead Technician ...**

His Cleveland readers saw a guy from Boston who wanted to head their way. That filled them with all sorts of skeptical thoughts: Why was he leaving his area? Would an Easterner like the Midwest? Would the Midwest like an Easterner? Could he possibly have any contacts in their locale? Would he be able to find his way around a new territory? Could he think like Midwesterners think? Would it cost them money to get him out here? What if his spouse didn't like it here?

Though George covered as many of these points as he could in his cover letter, he still didn't get the response he expected. He figured it had to be because, as an out-of-stater, he was perceived as a greater risk than in-state candidates. George needed to look local. And that was when his Aunt Sophie came into the picture. She was as Cleveland as you could get, and even had a street address in a prosperous suburb. George's third and final résumé looked like this:

GEORGE METCALF
18 Royal Oaks Road
Shaker Heights, OH 42256
(305) 877-4454

EXPERIENCE:
1989–Present   **Lead Technician...**

George was able to get his Aunt Sophie equipped with an answering machine with a message, recorded in her voice (as if she might be George's wife) that said: "Thank you for calling. We're away from the phone at the moment. Please leave a message for either George or me, and we'll get back to you as soon as possible."

It worked beautifully. Sophie would retrieve the message, call George in Boston right away, and he would return the call as if he were in the next county. At that point, if the issue came up, George had the company's ear and could explain how the move west would cause no problems. He even mentioned that he had family in the area.

Even Aunt Sophie enjoyed this process. It amused her to no end to raise a few eyebrows from friends when they heard her new taped message about this George fellow who seemed to be living with her!

29. Your Job Title Is Not Representative of What You Are

Job titles mean a lot to the reader. They are loaded with connotation, and you need to be careful that your title actually conveys the right message. For example, Executive Housekeeper for a hotel is a management position, not someone who makes beds. If an Executive Housekeeper were to try to promote his skills out of the hotel industry, his title would give the wrong impression.

If at all possible, manipulate your title to convey the proper message or connotation. Many companies give titles that don't accurately or fairly describe the scope of responsibility or technical capability of the employee. Check with your company to see if there would be any problem if you altered your official title to be more accurate or descriptive of your position. Make sure they will go along with the new title when a prospective employer calls to check references.

Another option is to list your official title and then, in parenthesis, to put your own, more descriptive and/or accurate title.

Sean Casper was an electronic engineer who specialized in design and design-modification work. He wanted to promote himself as a design engineer. His official title, however, was Electronic Technician—Level 2. It made him sound like a test technician rather than a design engineer, despite the fact that he did an enormous amount of design-engineering work. His company was large, and he was fearful their human resources department would simply "go by the book" and state only his official title. See how Sean changed part of his résumé:

SEAN'S RÉSUMÉ

PROFESSIONAL EXPERIENCE:
1985–Present

Arbitron Corporation   Burlington, MA
Promoted through several positions of increasing responsibility to the following design engineering position:

Electronic Technician (Level 2-**Engineering Design**) 2/91–present

Handle circuit modeling using Touchstone software. Supervise, provide technical advice, and delegate work to Engineering Assistants, including testing instructions and problem unit troubleshooting. Fully develop bid proposals. Provide technical guidelines for sales staff.

Design Work:
- Independently designed a successful filter for a subassembly that is currently in use. Drafted design on paper, then utilized Touchstone modeling, recruited an assembler to develop circuit, and personally tuned the design. Developed another filter for an oscillator with the same process.

- Currently working on a design for a prototype attenuator for German cable television. Modified existing design (using Touchstone software) to obtain proper performance specs.

Electronic Engineer Aide 2 (1988–1991)
- Worked independently and reported to staff and senior-level engineers.
- Handled multilevel testing and troubleshooting of subassemblies and logamps for customer evaluation prior to purchase.

Electronic Engineer Aide 1 (1986–1987)

Technician (1985–1986)

Notice that Sean emphasizes engineering design in several ways. After he has listed his company's name, he sets the stage by telling the reader that he has been promoted to a Design-Engineer position. Then he lists his official title, with no stylistic emphasis such as bolding, italic or underlining, and puts the important descriptive title in parenthesis and in bold. He continues to hammer home his design experience by adding a prominent subsection entitled Design Work.

Truly, Sean is a qualified designer of both circuits as well as good résumés.

30. You Have Several Job Objectives but Want Only One Résumé

Over the past 15 years, David Gabriella had used several professional skills and capabilities in three different environments. Now he was interested in developing a résumé that would be effective for any number of positions: Architect, Developer, Construction Project Manager, or a blend of all three. His problem was that his job history was not consistently in one of these areas. Some of his positions were with architectural firms, some with real estate developers, and some with construction firms. He didn't want a construction firm, for example, to read his résumé and label him as an architect. And he didn't want the architectural firm to label him as a construction project manager. Finally, he didn't want to develop several résumé versions because he felt that would be too confusing.

David felt strongly that his blend of talents would be an asset, so he developed a summary section in the beginning of his résumé that was in a menu format. It allowed his readers to understand his valuable blend of experience, and then to choose from the summary menu a particular area of interest, whether in architecture, construction and development, or project management. See David's "menu résumé" format on pages 113–114.

This format allowed David to use the benefits of both the functional (skills-oriented) and chronological (job history-oriented) résumé formats. It listed his skills in summary form, and then went on to job history to show the reader just where he got his particular experience. It allowed his readers to pick from the summary menu the particular experience they were looking for, and then it led them into his professional experience section to deliver more details.

Despite the fact that David's new résumé lacked an Objective section, he made it clear in the first two lines of his summary section that he was focused on applying his professional capabilities in the building industry in any or all of the three specific areas he'd listed. This effectively communicated his objective, yet gave him the flexibility of offering himself for any number of building industry positions. Further, he always wrote a focused cover letter that accompanied his résumé when he responded to specific opportunities.

DAVID'S "MENU RÉSUMÉ" FORMAT

DAVID E. GABRIELLA
91 Sotherby Road
Burlington, MA 02114
(617) 653-5532

SUMMARY:

Offer the benefits of a blend of 16 years of wide-ranging professional experience in the building industry. Significant capabilities include:

Architecture
- Registered Architect with award-winning designs.
- Solid background in production drawings, specifications, construction administration, and liability control.
- Design experience in a variety of building types: medical, corrections, R&D, academic, institutional, commercial.

Construction and Development
- Ground-up construction experience, from single-family wood frame through steel and concrete high-rise construction.
- Familiarity with the execution of architect's drawings and details in the field; an ability to improve contract documents.
- Experience in all phases of development from financial analysis and acquisition through construction and sales.

Project Management
- Demonstrated ability to manage large, complex projects with fast-track and design/build delivery systems.
- A take-charge approach, handling all facets of project management; hard-line negotiating

skills; an ability to communicate clearly and concisely with clients, colleagues, and consultants.

PROFESSIONAL EXPERIENCE:

Borson Associates, Inc.　　　Watertown, MA
Associate and Project Architect (1990–Present)
Manage the design and production process for design/build correctional projects. Project Architect for the Hanover County Jail and HCC, an $80M facility comprising 11 buildings and 700,000 square feet of program space. Supervise in-house CAD staff and contract consultants.

The Development Group　　　Melrose, MA
Director of Development (1986–1990)
Managed all North Shore projects for this Boston-based real estate development firm. Coordinated consultants, attained permits, designed facilities and managed construction, negotiated contracts.

Design Inc., Architects　　　Cambridge, MA
Project Manager (1982–1986)
Managed the design process for housing and office building types. Negotiated owner and consultant agreements, produced drawings and specifications, coordinated administration of contracts.

EDUCATION:

Massachusetts Institute of Technology
Master of Science in Architecture Studies (1982)
Bachelor of Architecture (1980)

PROFESSIONAL AWARDS:

First Award, Design Consultant: AI National Design Competition
First Award, Designer, Consultation Internationale, Paris, France

31. You've Been Self-Employed and Don't Want to Look That Way

Sometimes self-employment background doesn't sit well with prospective employers. The self-employed person is often prejudged as being set in his ways, unmoldable, and unable to follow a chain of command. Even worse, the entrepreneurial nature of the self-employed person is sometimes thought of by the prospective employer as a chronic problem, one which, as soon as opportunity knocks again, will pull this prospective employee back into self-employment. Even worse, there's often a fear that this person will ultimately become a competitor, forming his own company, and using his newly acquired tools, tactics, and competitive knowledge against his employer.

Ironically, self-employed people are often the hardest workers, the most highly self-educated in their field, and the most willing to wear any number of hats to get the job done. Despite this, self-employed people are often perceived as a threat.

If you find this to be the case, you may be better off swallowing your pride and giving yourself a title that best describes and matches the title of the position you're shooting for. Owner/Operator as a title never scores many points with a prospective employer. It sounds too "mom and pop" and gives the impression that the applicant is used to being the boss, not the one to be trained and follow orders.

If, for example, you've been self-employed and are looking for a management position, consider giving yourself the title General Manager rather than President or Owner.

If you have a specialized trade skill and have plied this trade within your own company, give yourself the title that best describes what you do and what you *want* to do. If, for example, you've been the owner/operator of a bakery, "owning" isn't really what you do or what you want to show you do. Your primary skill is probably baking and managing the baking process. So, if you're looking for a Manager/Head Baker position, make that your title.

This was the approach Janine Shardner took when she decided, after 12 years, to close her gourmet food shop and seek a management position in the food service industry. She knew she needed to take the self-employed flavor out of her résumé. See a part of Janine's résumé on the next page.

JANINE'S RÉSUMÉ

JANINE SHARDNER
86 Martin Square
Morristown, PA 55469
(935) 739-1633

OBJECTIVE: Management position in the food industry.

SUMMARY: Able to bring my employer extensive experience in a broad range of professional capabilities in the restaurant/food service field. Significant capabilities include:

- managing all aspects of profitable operations
- developing business through a variety of promotional methods
- providing the highest level of customer service/catering to a well-developed and loyal clientele
- utilizing knowledge of quality foods and cheeses
- applying knowledge gained from food product sales and distribution background servicing up to 200 accounts
- maintaining effective systems of cost and portion control
- developing and/or following standardized procedures and guidelines
- motivating and training staffs

RELEVANT EXPERIENCE:

1980–1992   Gourmet Stop   Morristown, PA
A light breakfast shop selling quality cheeses, whole bean coffees, in-store baked goods, and a sandwich/salad menu.

General Manager
Hands-on direction of all aspects of the Gourmet
Stop's business growth, operations, and
development of clientele.

Key Achievements: • Over a ten year period, led the business
through a period of 18% compounded
growth per year...

In her summary section, Janine has set the right tone by
deferring to her prospective employer, stating that she is "able to
bring my employer extensive experience..." This line places the
emphasis on Janine as an employee, not an owner who is used to
running her own show. She goes on to list the broad range of skills
and benefits she would bring to an employer.

Notice that in her job description for the Gourmet Stop Janine
doesn't mention anywhere that she was the owner, only that she "led
the business through a period of 18% compounded growth per
year," something that any employer would want a manager to do.
She gives herself the title of General Manager, which is what she
really was—and what her prospective employer really wants!

A final note: If your situation is such that there is no way you
can't show self-employment—for example, your business name is
your last name, you're job seeking in a geographical area where you
and your business have been well known, you fear that being
unclear about your business ownership on your résumé will ultimately be detrimental at the interview or later on in your new
job—an effective approach is to use the following line in your cover
letter:

My experience running and growing a business has taught me that
there are no short cuts to success; hard work and long hours
come with the territory. I look forward to applying these same work
ethics within your company.

32. You Worked for the Same Company Two Different Times in Your Career

You can make this work to your advantage. This type of experience will often be perceived as a positive, for it shows one good thing: You must have been a valued employee because your company hired you back.

As a general rule, the fewer jobs you show on your résumé the better. So, in a case where you've had the same employer on two occasions, list the overall dates of employment in the left margin, and then the specific dates of each position after each of your job titles. Don't list the company twice, as Anthony Peraldi did in his first résumé. When read quickly, it gave the impression that he'd had three employers in four years. It looked like this:

ANTHONY'S FIRST RÉSUMÉ

PROFESSIONAL EXPERIENCE:

1992–Present	Seven Seas Ship & Fish Supply Gloucester, MA **Manager**—Wholesale Department Manage daily operations of wholesale fish department including purchasing and sales operations, pricing, gross profit analysis, new account and supplier development, direct sales, staff hiring, and training.
Key Achievements:	• Managed growth from @ $350K to $1.2 million over 5 years. • Developed major accounts such as Foley Fish, Steve Connolly Seafoods, Legal Seafoods, Great Eastern Seafoods.
1990–1991	Newburyport Fish Company Newburyport, MA **General Manager** Responsibilities included new account development, managing financial operations,

and overseeing the processing side of the business.
- Managed company growth from 0 to @ $350K.
- Developed new accounts that included major area restaurants.

1989–1990   Seven Seas Ship & Fish Supply   Gloucester, MA
Assistant Manager—Marine Retail Department
Maintained responsibility for operations within the commercial and recreational marine end of the corporation. Was active in retail buying, pricing, promotions, and sales.
- Played an important role in department's growth from @ $750K to $2.2 million over 5 years.

Anthony's new résumé, a part of which is shown on page 120, clearly indicates just two employers, and progressive experience with his current company. In the left margin he's listed both periods of employment with Seven Seas Ship & Fish Supply. Then he's lumped both jobs under one company heading. This frees up several lines and allows him to list more achievements, because it eliminates the need to repeat the company heading with each period of employment. Further, it gives the impression of progressive, continuous, and hence more valuable experience with one employer, rather than indicating shorter-term, segmented experience, as his old résumé did. With his new résumé, Anthony was well equipped to hook a new employer.

ANTHONY'S NEW RÉSUMÉ

EXPERIENCE:

1992–Present,
1989–1990

Seven Seas Ship & Fish Supply   Gloucester, MA
Manager—Wholesale Department (1992–present)
Manage daily operations of wholesale fish
department, including purchasing and sales
operations, pricing, gross profit analysis, new
account and supplier development, direct
sales, staff hiring, and training.

Key Achievements:
- Managed growth from @ $350K to $1.2 million over 5 years.
- Developed major accounts such as Foley Fish, Steve Connolly Seafoods, Legal Seafoods, Great Eastern Seafoods.
- Opened and managed new accounts beyond Boston/North Shore to Philadelphia and New York.

Assistant Manager—Marine Department
(1989–1990)
Maintained responsibility for operations within
the commercial and recreational marine end
of the corporation. Was active in retail buying,
pricing, promotions, and sales.

- Played an important role in department's growth from @ $750K to $2.2 million over 5 years.

1990–1991

Newburyport Fish Company   Newburyport, MA
General Manager
Responsibilities included new account
development, managing financial operations,
and overseeing the processing side of the
business.

- Managed company growth from 0 to @ $350K.
- Developed new accounts which included major area restaurants.

---

33. You Are Working Two Jobs and Don't Know Whether to Show Them Both

When you have a question about whether to put something in or leave something out of your résumé, put yourself in the shoes of the reader. Think in terms of the need and greed of your prospective employer.

What would your reaction be if you were a prospective employer reading a résumé listing two concurrent jobs? At first thought, you might expect the employer to respond: "Wow, this applicant is a very hard worker."

But if you really think about the need and greed of the person who is going to be hiring you—the person who is going to be paying you *his* money each week to work for *him* handling responsibilities for *his* company—then the reaction is more likely to be this: "This applicant must be worn thin by having to balance the schedule and demands of two jobs. This is a full-time, demanding position I have to fill. I need someone to work for me and me alone. I don't want to share my employee with some other company."

It is often best to list only one position when you are working two. And it is best to list the position that shows the experience most pertinent to your reader. Even if that position is part time, there's no rule that says you must list it as such on your résumé. Simply list the most pertinent of your two positions as your "relevant experience," date it, describe it in the most relevant way possible, and list any achievements associated with that position.

Your prospective employer will be glad to see the quality of your contribution, not the quantity of your employers!

34. Your Résumé Looks Like Words, Words, Words

Give it some style!

Take your résumé to someone who has a laser printer that can style your résumé with such things as bolding, italics, different point sizes, and bullets. Ask yourself: What words do I want to draw the reader's attention to? Which words carry the most meaning and value for the reader? These are the words that should be emphasized with bold, italic, or underlining. Many people inappropriately emphasize category headings (*Education, Experience, Objective,* etc.). These words do absolutely nothing to enhance the value of the candidate. If it's your title you want the reader to see, emphasize that. If it's the name of the company, emphasize that. If it's a particular degree or certification, emphasize that. A word of caution: Don't overemphasize or over-style. The purpose of styling is to draw the readers' eyes to a particular word or phrase. Too much bold or italic print defeats the purpose.

Make a list of the highest-priority areas of your background. Which is the #1 point you want your reader to see? Which is #2? And so forth. Your strongest emphasis should be on these points, in order of their importance.

Study Each Word You've Written for Value or Redundancy

Shorten your paragraphs by reducing impotent lead-in phrases. For example, "Maintained responsibility for directing..." can be shortened to "Directed..." Likewise, "Position required the use of computer skills..." can be shortened to "Used computer skills..."

Avoid Big Block Paragraphs

They use up white space, appear burdensome, and turn off the reader. Job descriptions form the biggest blocks of text, yet they are the least-read part of any résumé. Readers concentrate on titles, specialized skills, and achievements. Don't waste words or space on

BARBARA'S RÉSUMÉ

BARBARA A. CARSON
633 South Street
South Dartmouth, MA 01923
(508) 249-4761

OBJECTIVE: Elementary level teaching position.

- B.S., Elementary Education, *summa cum laude*.
- Recipient of 100% "outstanding" ratings on student teaching report.
- Training and experience in integrated learning and textbook approaches.
- Solid computer background. Experience teaching computer functions and using computers to facilitate learning in all subject areas.
- Highly creative and effective integrated learning lesson planner.
- A maturity gained from five years of professional business experience.

"Kathleen is a tireless, inspiring, creative person. Children love her. Prediction of success: excellent."   1992 Student Teaching Report

**TEACHING
EXPERIENCE:**

Gossman School   Marion, MA
Student Teacher—Grade 2 (1/92–5/92)
Trained under Mary Fox, a highly experienced elementary teacher.

Key Contributions:

- Effectively integrated computer into writing workshop; students worked in cooperative learning groups to write fictional stories.

- Integrated reading with math through use of the book <u>The Oxcart Man</u>; students learned the concept of borrowing and carrying through the borrowing and carrying metaphor of the fruit cart vendor.

- Developed an Earth Day acid rain experiment that informed students of pollution problems and the chemical impact of acid rain.

Horace Mann School   So. Boston, MA
Student Teacher—<u>Whole Language Classroom</u> (1991)
Assisted in a whole language classroom under John Roberts.
- Taught an integrated learning unit on Thanksgiving that integrated grammar (teaching the value and use of subjects, predicates, and verbs).

EDUCATION: Salem State College, **B.S., Elementary Education**, 5/92
Minor: Business Administrative Services
Honors: *summa cum laude*. G.P.A.: 3.87

CERTIFICATION: Elementary Education, Massachusetts, 5/92

OTHER EXPERIENCE: The Dance Workshop of Marion   Marion, MA
Assisted owner and instructor with dance classes for children (1989).

Stone Properties, Inc.   Attleboro, MA
Full Charge Bookkeeper—<u>Computerized Systems</u> (1986–1988)
- Given consistently increasing responsibility from entry bookkeeping to assisting the Chief Financial Officer.
- Recipient of several *Outstanding Performance Awards*.

the obvious parts of your job description. For example, if you're an airline Flight Attendant, you don't need to say "Responsible for serving the needs and attending to the safety and comfort of passengers." Your readers already know that. Instead, you should concentrate on showing any special skills, training, or achievements that *enhance* your value as a Flight Attendant. You can do this by using bullets, which will make your résumé much more interesting visually and give you more white space. Be sure not to overdo; too many bullets are self-defeating because they run together and lose visual impact. See Barbara's résumé on pages 123–124 for an example of a thoughtfully styled and therefore powerful résumé.

Notice how Barbara Carson's résumé is interesting. It has personality. It has a certain flavor. Throughout the résumé she has sprinkled in bold face, italics, and underlining to draw her readers toward certain job or educational highlights. She has prioritized what she wants her readers to see. Her #1 priority is "summa cum laude," so she makes sure it's styled in a way that gets attention. She wants her readers to see her review from her 1992 Student Teaching Report, so she puts this in italics. She was proud of her "key contributions" during her student teaching at the Gossman School, so she places them in their own subcategory in the middle of the résumé. They clearly show her creativity as a lesson planner and teacher. Further, under Stone Properties Barbara has underlined Computerized Systems. She wants to show her professional career work with computers because that experience will be an asset in the classroom. Finally, she wants to show the quality of her performance with Stone Properties, so she highlights Outstanding Performance Awards.

Clearly, Barbara will be a good teacher. And one with style!

35. You Don't Know What Personal Information to Include on Your Résumé

The rule of thumb is this: If putting any of these categories into your résumé may help *but can't possibly hurt*, then you're safe. Look into each category and ask yourself: is there any value there?

Examples:

Personal Interest, Affiliations, and Community Activities

Any interests or affiliations you list should have value to the reader. Be sure you know the needs, culture, and interests of your audience before you list any interests or affiliations that have strong connotations. Don't otherwise assume your reader will relate to your specific interests. That can backfire. For example, indicating that you're a motorcycle club member may not sit well with an environmentally conscious employer. Mentioning your contributions to the Democratic presidential campaign won't gain you an interview with a Republican reader. Stay away from political or religious affiliations unless those are the areas of your job objective and you know your audience.

The interests or affiliations you list should somehow reinforce your ability to meet the needs of your job objective as well as match the culture of the prospective company and/or industry. For example, if you're a high-level sales professional in an industry that begins many of its deals on the golf course, then listing golf as an interest would most likely be perceived as an asset.

Professional affiliations that indicate you have strong industry contacts and specialized knowledge can be an asset. Sometimes community affiliations can have the same value, depending on your industry and vocation. Don't list too many, however. A list that is too long makes you look like a "committee person" who spends more time on committees than at work.

If you have a hobby that, by its very nature, reinforces your work skills, then you should list it. *Examples:* a travel guide who reads history as a hobby; a restaurant manager who enjoys gourmet cooking at home; an office manager who enjoys home computer applications.

Marital Status and Age

It's against the law for a prospective employer to ask your age or marital status. Don't put either on your résumé. And don't try to second-guess your prospective employer's desire for single or married employees. It can backfire. Sometimes single people list their marital status on the résumé because they think that being single will be viewed as an asset because they have more freedom to travel and fewer personal encumbrances. Likewise married people sometimes list their marital status because they think that being married shows stability and a sense of commitment to an employer because of family obligations. The fact is that it's anybody's guess how the employer will see things. So don't guess. Leave it alone.

Do not list your date of birth. If you feel your early career makes you look too much like a relic, then don't go that far back in your job history. There's no rule that says you must list all your employment history on your résumé. Go back only as far as is relevant (and include those dates). If you have a degree and you don't want to list your date of graduation because it reveals your age, at least be consistent by omitting *all* dates from the Education section. The reader may wonder why there are no dates in that section, but he won't know for sure why you left them out, and it shouldn't be a cause to lose the interview opportunity. (Leaving your dates of employment out may cause you to lose an interview, however.)

Military Experience

Again, if something in your military career supports your objective—perhaps it was specialized training, a particular skill you learned, or any awards that demonstrate your competence or ability to perform—then you should consider listing military experience. If it has no bearing on your objective, leave it out.

36. There's a Gap in Your Employment History

You have several options here. If your gap is not a large one, simply list whole years rather than months and years. This was Harold Lister's problem:

HAROLD'S FIRST RÉSUMÉ

PROFESSIONAL EXPERIENCE:

9/91–Present

Beach Way Cosmetics   Danvers, MA
Retail Store Accounting
Provide a wide range of support services, from sorting mail to weekly payroll, accounts payable, petty cash management, and monthly/quarterly sales and payroll taxes for this successful retail operation.
• Significantly reduced company's accountant's bill.
• Set up a mailing system for store promotions and marketing.

7/90–2/91

Resource Telecommunications   Boston, MA
Office/Accounting Manager
Similar accounting responsibilities as those listed in above position, in addition to excise tax returns and overall supervision of a 24-hour per day staff of up to 25.
• Streamlined accounting operations, consolidated books, and discovered excess charges that effected considerable savings for the corporation.

4/88–1/90

Systems Plus, Inc.   Marblehead, MA
General Manager
Developed this . . .

Harold had a seven-month gap and a six-month gap between his periods of employment. Those gaps disappeared when he took the months out of his new résumé:

HAROLD'S NEW RÉSUMÉ

PROFESSIONAL EXPERIENCE:

1991–Present	Beach Way Cosmetics Danvers, MA

Retail Store Accounting
Provide a wide range of support services, from sorting mail to weekly payroll, accounts payable, petty cash management, and monthly/quarterly sales and payroll taxes for this successful retail operation.
- Significantly reduced company's accountant's bill.
- Set up a mailing list system for store promotions and marketing.

1990–1991	Resource Telecommunications Boston, MA

Office/Accounting Manager
Similar accounting responsibilities as those listed in above position, in addition to excise tax returns and overall supervision of a 24-hour per day staff of up to 25.
- Streamlined accounting operations, consolidated books, and discovered excess charges that effected considerable savings for the corporation.

1988–1990	Systems Plus, Inc. Marblehead, MA

General Manager
Developed this . . .

If your gap is bigger than a year, ask yourself what you did during that period that was of value. Did you continue your education? Did you independently consult? Did you do any independent projects that enhanced your skills? Did you raise children? Did you volunteer? Did you manage the care of a sick relative?

My point is this: Don't be afraid to come clean and state some productive project or contribution to fill in any gap in your employment history.

See below for an example of what Anne Delacorte did with her résumé after she received feedback that her gap of two years between her two major professional positions was hurting her.

ANNE'S RÉSUMÉ

PROFESSIONAL EXPERIENCE

Borten Corporation, Waltham, MA   1991–1992

A leading manufacturer and seller of specialized software that enables developers to rapidly create high-performance business applications for open systems.

District Manager/Senior Sales Representative
- 100% prospecting in New England, New York City, and Central Northwest.
- Organized joint participation with Digital in VAR/OEM seminar.
- Developed Borten/Digital relationship through direct sales presentations to Digital field sales offices.
- Developed Fortune 500 accounts through 100% prospecting, including seminars and presentations.

Continuing Education—Harvard   1989–1990

Entrex, Incorporated, Cambridge, MA   1983–1988

A leading developer, manufacturer, and marketer of object-oriented programming for software development on networked workstations.

Senior Sales Representative

Increasing responsibility for sales territories in the Greater Boston area. Initial assignment included 100% prospecting in a defined geographic territory with progression to national account development and management.

- Earned "High Achiever" status by exceeding 115% of annual sales goals, which increased from $1.2 million to $2 million.

Anne's experience with Entrex had been highly successful but also highly stressful. She'd made an enormous amount of money in commissions, but at the end of 1988 she badly needed a break from the road and some time for personal growth. True, during this break she traveled quite a bit and took it easy, but she also studied both business and liberal arts at Harvard. So she spliced a reference to this into her Professional Experience section. Doing this didn't seem to threaten the continuity of her work experience too much, since she made only brief reference to it as a way to fill in the gap. She went on to explain the details of that educational experience in another category, thereby preserving the continuity of her Professional Experience section.

Putting It All Together— What Makes the Résumé Work

The résumé's primary job is to be persuasive. Think of your résumé as a snapshot of your value to the job market. Like any good snapshot, it must be focused and appealing. Your initial approach in developing your résumé is critical. Step outside yourself and look back. Change roles. Put yourself in the place of the reader. If you were the potential employer, what would you want to see? What pieces of your background would help you get hired? Put those pieces in. And what parts of your past would lessen your chances of getting the job? Leave those pieces out. Write the résumé for the need and greed of the reader, not for yourself. Ask yourself the four questions from Winning Move #14: What do you want? Why are you qualified to do it? Where have you done it? How well have you done it?

Give your résumé the ultimate value test: Think of it as a piece of paper blowing along the sidewalk of a busy street. What is going to make the reader pick it up? What will grab the reader's eye? What separates it from all other sheets whirling around him? Make your résumé worth the reader's time and effort. Show value. Be persuasive, not timid. Be colorful, not bland. Paint an alluring picture of your value by concentrating on achievements and specific capabilities, not by wasting space on job descriptions and responsibilities that are obvious. Give it flavor and uniqueness by showing specific instances of how you've helped your employer.

Make your résumé visually inviting. Keep as much white space as possible. Don't crowd the page. Have it laser-printed by someone who will maintain the data file for easy updating and editing. Use a high-quality paper. Skip the wild colors. And have at least two other people—including a colleague, if possible—read your résumé for typos, grammar, and content.

Finally, don't let the résumé format make you uptight. Relax and let your value points flow, the way you would when bragging to a friend. Don't worry about length at first. Get all the valuable material down and then begin to cut out what is redundant, not applicable, or not so persuasive. As you would when framing a good snapshot, show only what needs to be shown, then focus and shoot.

As Winning Moves #16 to 36 show, there's always a solution to your résumé dilemma. And as the ancient proverb says, where there is no solution, there is no dilemma.

The Cover Letter: Just a Line Won't Get You in the Door— You'll Need a Hook as Well

The function of the cover letter is, first and foremost, to get the reader's attention. To receive a résumé with no personal statement of intent "covering" the résumé is in all cases awkward. Many recipients consider people who don't send a cover letter downright rude. A cover letter is the knock on the door before entering. It's the "How are you?" before the "May I borrow your car?" It's both good manners and a formality. And the truly effective cover letters are those that hook the reader on what is to follow: you.

Let's start with some basic premises about the people who receive your unsolicited broadcast/cover letters: They don't know you; they didn't ask to know you; they are busy; and they may think they don't need you or anybody. Tough start. Don't give up. They're all hungry—they just need the right bait.

The bait is the lead of your letter. And I don't mean the kind of lead you may think of using. "Enclosed please find . . ." or "I am writing in regard to . . ." are leads which (a) waste valuable first-line opportunity, (b) don't communicate any value about you, and (c) look like everybody else's (yawn).

A Lead That Gets Attention

"In the past ten years I've been in Sing Sing Prison twenty-two times." That sentence got your attention, didn't it? Such a lead (the writer went on to say he was a prison system auditor looking for a position) may be an exaggerated example, but it worked. And that is critical.

I recently received two pieces of unsolicited mail with leads that hooked me. One was from an office administrator who'd read about me in the paper. I'd been quoted as saying my company was growing and that was great, but I was becoming more and more of an administrator, and I didn't like that part. Her letter's lead: "Congratulations on the growth of your company. Growth is exciting, except for the administrative part, as you said in the paper last week. Well, that is my specialty! I'm an administrator who can relieve you of just those burdens you outlined."

"Welcome!" I said when she followed up with her phone call.

The other piece of mail came to my home and was from a trash compactor bag company. It was a cheaply produced but properly targeted solicitation asking me if I was "tired of having my compactor bags rip and spill all over my feet and floor." I was. The hook was baited properly. I went for the bags.

Communicate value in your lead. It will hook the reader. *Examples:*

With Global Enterprises I increased Southeast Territory sales by 42 percent in one year. I would like the opportunity to do the same for your company.

If Jason Ski Wear needs a creative boost for its outdoor line, my achievements with Skyline Ski Wear may be of interest to you.

You may have received lots of inquiries regarding positions as a photographer's assistant at Photo Studios, but perhaps you've heard from no one who could...

Perhaps Asaki America could benefit from a Project Manager who has lived and studied in Japan and has professional experience in automated systems design.

As a highly experienced Materials Management professional (MRP), my expertise and career commitment has been to reduce inventory, lead time, staffing, and costs. I've done this consistently throughout my career and I am currently seeking the right opportunity to do it again.

A Body That Keeps It

The body of your letter—the second paragraph—should contain just enough valuable information about your professional abilities to keep the reader's interest. If you have a skill that is particularly well matched for the job, that should be mentioned here, even though it will also be mentioned in your résumé. The second or third paragraphs are also good places to drop a few industry buzz words in order to quickly show that you're in the right league.

Give the body of your letter enough substance to hold the reader.

For example:

Over the past 15 years, as a Director of Materials and as a Manufacturing Manager for Analogic and Sanders Associates respectively, I have been remarkably successful in critical MRP areas. In fact, I have consistently attained my ambitious reduction goals in dramatically shorter periods of time than expected.

Perhaps it is my high level of energy and love of what I do that has made me effective. Whatever the reason, if issues of reduction of inventory, lead time, staffing, and costs are on your list of priorities, I believe a review of my enclosed list of capabilities and accomplishments would be worth your time.

A Close That Leaves the Door Open

Close your letter in a way that keeps the ball rolling and offers a taste of more to come, as the author of the following closing paragraph has done:

I certainly would welcome the opportunity to "talk shop" regarding particular challenges within your company, and to discuss how my skills and ideas may be a valuable addition. I look forward to meeting at your convenience.

Finally, always keep your cover letter to one page. And be sure to follow up as close as possible to the time your reader is likely to receive your letter. Don't sit back and wait for a response. For more information on specific follow-up techniques, see Winning Move #11 in the Marketing section. Winning Move #47 in the Shining Examples section gives a detailed example of one writer's irresistible cover letter.

Winning Move #38:
Read Between the Lines
of Help-Wanted Ads

Though help-wanted ads don't account for a major part of the job market, they are still a source of opportunity. I should say that *some* are a source of opportunity. It's important to be able to sense whether an ad truly represents a good opportunity. Responding to help-wanted ads that misrepresent the actual situation can quickly demoralize a job seeker.

It's important to understand that there are numerous reasons for help-wanted ads:

- Legally, the company may be required to advertise the job (even though the job is already spoken for).
- Politically, the company may feel it looks best to advertise the job (even though the job is already spoken for).
- The ad may not be placed by the company at all, but by a headhunter; the headhunter may have an actual position or he may be looking to draw client companies by collecting a certain type of candidate.
- The job may not be a job at all, but a "business opportunity" veiled as a job. The ad may be designed to draw a potential clientele from the ranks of unsuspecting job seekers.

Some Rules of Thumb About Answering Help-Wanted Ads

Beware of the "Too Good to Be True" Ad—It Usually Is

> Highly successful and dynamic company seeks a motivated, take-charge individual who has the desire for high earnings and the discipline to work hard in managing the sales function. If you're that individual, and own your own car, get your résumé to us fast, or call us at . . .

This position is most likely a pure-commission, cold-call sales job with no benefits, little or no training, a slim commission structure, and no equipment support (no company-supplied vehicle).

The More Demanding and Specific the Ad, the Better the Job

> Sales Manager—small, growing North Shore firm seeks a sales manager with at least five years of sales-management experience, a college degree, and direct experience in the set-up and management of a distributor network. Please submit résumé with a cover letter explaining why you'd be effective in the position. Excellent base salary plus incentives.

The tone of the ad tells us that this is a self-assured company that has a serious position of value. Notice that the company doesn't try to sell the candidate on how great it is. They will pay well, but they obviously aren't willing to compromise on the background they want. They don't invite phone calls. And they want to assess the candidate's written communication skills via the cover letter. If you're qualified, apply for this position and give them what they want.

Your Salary History Is No One's Business but Your Own

When a company requests your salary history as a part of your written response to its help-wanted advertisement, they are saying, in essence, that they will be making a judgment about you based on what people paid you. Is that right? What if you were underpaid? Overpaid? Or worked in a different region of the country with a different cost of living?

It is certainly not the business of a stranger from a strange company who is not yet your employer (or even your prospective employer) to know the history of your compensation. Besides, both you and any of your prospective employers should already know the market value of the level of your position. As the job seeker, your goal is to generate a face-to-face meeting or interview, and *then* deal with compensation. No one wants to be eliminated before he gets a chance to compete.

If you feel you might be eliminated if you don't respond to the request for salary history, try to respond in a subjective, non-specific manner. For example:

My salary history over the past decade has followed the industry norm. At times, due to my performance, it has exceeded that norm. I will be pleased to provide further details upon our meeting...

Give Them a Range When They Ask for Salary Requirements

One of the most common dilemmas facing the job seeker who responds to a help-wanted ad is the salary requirements question. On the one hand, you don't want to lose an opportunity for an interview because of too high a salary request. On the other hand, a figure that is too low could cost you thousands of dollars.

One of the best ways to respond to a help-wanted ad that requests salary requirements is to provide the prospective employer with a range. If, for example, you wish or need to make $57,000 per year, you might write the following:

My salary requirement is in the 50s, and is both reasonable and negotiable, depending on the company's type of compensation plan.

This manner of response gives the job seeker a fairly safe salary range, for the prospective employer isn't sure if the requirement is for the low, mid, or high 50s.

Time Your Follow-up to Coincide with the Moment They Read Your Letter

Unless the advertiser requests "no phone calls," follow up while the letter and résumé are still fresh in the mind of the reader. Waiting too long is a risk; your mailing may have already been forgotten, filed, misfiled, or routed to the human resources department. Following up too soon is not a risk; the worst that can happen is that you'll have a preliminary conversation with a prospective employer. You'll get a chance to score a few points before he receives the résumé. Plus, he'll know it's coming.

Beware the Blind Ad

Blind ads are those that don't list the name of your prospective employer. Blind ads are tough. You can't do research on the company. You can't follow up by telephone to sell yourself or push for an interview. You can only wait. The ball is in the prospective employer's court.

And there is always the ultimate danger: A job-seeking electrical engineer I knew actually responded to his own job! He was called into the boss's office the following Monday and there on the desk was the engineer's résumé. "I see you and I have similar thoughts about your future here," the boss said, looking down at the résumé. Needless to say, the engineer soon found that he had plenty of time to intensify his job search.

So be careful of blind ads, especially if you feel that any industry awareness that you're job seeking could jeopardize your position.

Whom Does It Concern?

If the advertisement doesn't give the name of the person to whom you should respond, the safest way to write the cover letter salutation is "Dear Sir/Madam." "To whom it may concern" sounds cold and impersonal. "Dear Sir" is very dangerous—don't assume it's a man to whom you're responding. If there's a name listed but it's hard to tell the sex of the person ("please respond to S. Hennick"), the best approach is "Dear S. Hennick."

Help-wanted ads are somewhat of a crap shoot. Typically, they account for less than 10 percent of an area's hiring market. But 10 percent is still 10 percent, so they're worth a shot. But don't let them demoralize you. Understand your odds. Read the ads carefully. Analyze them. Respond to those that seem real. And follow up whenever possible.

Don't Let Headhunters
Go to Your Head

If headhunters find you tasty, you probably don't need them, unless you are a hopelessly ineffective job seeker and self-promoter. The fact that one or many headhunters find you immediately appealing usually means that the job market will also find you immediately appealing. If the market finds you appealing, you should have no difficulty selling yourself without the aid of a headhunter.

A headhunter gets paid by the company that hires you. You do not pay the headhunter. (Stay away from any agencies that want a placement fee up front from you, the job seeker.) Because a headhunter's time is money, he will not waste any of it on you unless he sees value. Headhunters do not earn a cent from counseling you, from rewriting your résumé, or from giving advice. Hence, they will usually get to the bottom line quickly about whether or not they want to work with you. Generally speaking, headhunters are paid a fee that is a percentage (usually between 15 percent and 30 percent) of your first year's gross salary.

Selling yourself through a headhunter is like selling a house through a broker: you net less money because the broker's fee is tacked on. If you independently sell yourself into a company that also uses headhunters, you may be in a much better bargaining position. For example, if your salary requirement is $60,000 and a headhunter gets you the interview, the company that hires you will be on the hook for at least 20 percent ($12,000). Because of this the company may try to cover their placement fee costs by offering you $50,000. Conversely, you'll have much more bargaining leverage if you approach the company on your own, with no fee attached.

This is not to say that headhunters don't serve a purpose. They do. They make it their business to know certain markets, and they can cut through the red tape and screening within companies to get their clients interviews. Well-reputed headhunters have strong client–company relationships; hence, when they recommend a candidate, the candidate will usually get an interview.

Like help-wanted ads, headhunters do account for a part of the hiring market. But also as with help-wanted ads, they shouldn't be relied upon as the sole source of job leads.

The best way to contact headhunters is to send them a résumé with a short cover letter stating your intent. You don't need to try to persuade them to work with you. They're pros who will scan your résumé and make an immediate assessment as to your value to them. Believe me, if they see a match, they'll call you. If they don't, they won't. Following up with a telephone call can't hurt, though. Perhaps they can provide you with some valuable industry information or trends.

The best source of information—it lists headhunters and their specialties—is the comprehensive *Directory of Executive Recruiters*, published by Kennedy Publications in Fitzwilliam, New Hampshire. You can order it by phone: (603) 585–6544.

Interviewing: Shoot First and You Won't Get Killed

The job interview is a stressful, artificial, stilted, agonizing, and inevitable situation. But it is also a plateau near the summit. Though the air is thin up there, it's only because you're almost at the top. Don't fall. The odds are with you at this point because most likely the interviewer *wants to like you*. You've made the cut. You're probably up against several others now, rather than several hundred others during the résumé-screening stage. The company is hoping you're the perfect candidate. They've already made a choice that you're worth their time to interview. Let's not disappoint them.

Here's How You, as Supercandidate, Outpoint Your Fellow Interviewees

You Know Them Better Than They Know You

There's nothing worse than having to say to the interviewer halfway through the interview, "By the way, just what is it you people do here?"

By studying Winning Move #10 and applying those research techniques, you learn more about your prospective employer. By knowing more about the company at which you'll be interviewing, you're more confident and less anxious, knowing you'll encounter fewer surprises. And you're able to ask intelligent questions. If nothing else, just showing that knowledge at the interview will impress the interviewer and score points.

You've done your research. You've learned about the company's products or services. You know their position in the market. You know their strong and weak points. You also know which strengths and weaknesses about yourself you'll want to show or hide.

You Know What They Are Likely to Ask You

You know what goods the company has on you. They have your résumé. They've probably studied it. They've probably made either written or mental notes about your strengths, value, and potential weaknesses. What might these be? You think about what you know about them and their potential needs and then look into your résumé with a critical eye. You anticipate their concerns based on what skills of yours may not match their needs. You write out what your responses would be to these concerns. By writing these responses, you cement them into your memory. You counter any objections or design "bridge responses," ones that take you over the voids of the simple negative answer.

Example: The interviewer might ask if you know how to run a Macintosh computer. You don't. But you won't say that. Saying "no" will lose points. Instead, you'll bridge your response to a positive by saying, "Well, I've gained extensive experience on an IBM PC with a variety of programs. Learning the Mac would be no problem—an easy transition, I would imagine, from the IBM."

So prior to the interview you've already anticipated and practiced responding to the worst-case scenarios. You feel good about that. And you're ready, like a good politician, to talk your way around the weak spots.

You Dress for the Occasion

It's the day of the interview. You're going into the interview radiating self-confidence. Why not? You are what you are and you've done everything you could to prepare. You've scheduled the interview to allow you time to exercise first; this has offset your excess adrenaline. You're calm. Your mind is sharp. Any food you've eaten is well digested prior to the interview because you want your blood in your brain, not busy digesting food in your growling stomach.

You've dressed conservatively and neatly, because by doing so you know you minimize the risk of offending anyone's tastes by looking too stylish or offbeat. There's a reason "classic" clothing doesn't fall out of favor. And if you wear it you increase the odds that you won't fall out of favor either. Besides, you don't want your clothes to be making the statement; *you* want to be making the statement. And you know you can change your statement when you meet the interviewer; you can't change your purple flowered tie. So you don't try to second-guess the tastes of the person with whom you're interviewing. Also, you're conservative in fragrance, makeup, and hairstyle. You know that, unless you have a very clear understanding of the company's culture and dress code, it's best to play it safe. Finally, remembering when Murphy's Law usually strikes, you bring along an extra blouse or shirt and tie. The one time you'll spill coffee on yourself will be on the day of the interview.

I remember a horror story a client once told me. He was so worried about a shaving cut on his neck that he'd covered it with his finger during his interview. His adrenaline got flowing. His finger got to rubbing. The cut reopened. Blood pumped. He fidgeted. Blood dripped onto his white shirt. He squirmed in his chair. He fidgeted and scratched his forehead with his bloody fingers, adding another red blotch to his brow. In short, he was a mess. Finally, it was the interviewer who could stand it no longer; he suggested the candidate take a few moments to go clean himself up.

You Arrive with Time to Spare

To further lessen your anxiety, you get there early, giving yourself an hour's cushion. Because you're there early you get to look around. You scope out the place. You don't drink the coffee offered you. Instead you try to talk to some employees or read some company literature. You notice things; this will give you more to talk about when you first meet the interviewer. And you don't sit down while waiting. You stand. If you're nervous, say to yourself such things as: "This is not a life or death situation," or "This person interviewing me is just another person and was once on my side of the desk getting interviewed."

You're Ready for the Interview

When the interviewer comes to greet you, you're up and alert. Active. Ready. Not a sloucher. You give a firm handshake and smack the interviewer with a big SMILE. You're glad to be there. It's an opportunity. Your smile is a calming and relaxing gesture, taking you closer to your first goal of relaxing the interview to make it more productive. Then you'll climb right into the interview, showing interest, enthusiasm, and a desire to learn more about the company and the position.

Get Involved. Show Your Interest. Ask Questions. The Goal Is to "Talk Shop" as Quickly as Possible

You might say: "I've done some research about your company and the position you're trying to fill and I'm enthusiastic, but I would love to know more. What are the key challenges of the position? How would you see my role in meeting these challenges?"

You don't count on your interviewer being skilled, knowing that most are not professional interviewers, but professionals who have to interview. They may not know how to ask the right questions. They may not know how to assess your value to them. It's up to you to help them. Getting them to talk about their needs will allow you to hand-feed them your value and benefit. The sooner you can get the interviewer to do this, the sooner you're able to show how your particular strengths can help fill those needs. The interviewer is flattered when asked questions about his or her company, the challenges ahead, and the goals the company wishes to attain. You know that if you don't learn their needs and goals, you'll only be guessing which abilities or skills you should emphasize.

Avoid Clichés Like the Plague

When you're asked a question, you don't answer in a general, clichéd manner. You provide evidence for your responses. For example, if the interviewer asks you: "Why do you think you can get us to the point of dominant market share by year-end?" you don't say, "Because I'm a can-do, results-oriented kind of guy." In making your response, you draw a picture, giving them something to hang onto. You might say: "When I was with Widget, Inc., I met the same sort of challenge, getting our widgets into 44 Whopping Widget Centers in 23 states. I did it by..."

Since you've spent a lot of time in the interview talking shop, the interviewer hasn't gotten to or bothered with the standardized questions, so you haven't had to worry about these. It's a good idea to formulate answers, however, to these classics.

"Tell Me About Yourself" Is the Lazy Interviewer's Trump Card

You'll know others when you hear them: "Where do you see yourself in five years?" "Why did you leave your last job?" "What is your greatest weakness?" Many books on interviewing will bombard you with lists of commonly asked questions, followed by paragraph after paragraph of "best responses." The problem is that if you take these questions to heart, your brain will be crammed with worries about a huge number of mental scripts you've written to respond to all these questions. The prepared-response approach rarely works; even if the right data comes out of your mouth it often sounds stilted. Often panic sets in while the brain searches for the prepared answer, when ironically the most impressive answer is the spontaneous one. Better not to worry. Be yourself. Don't be afraid to pause and gather your thoughts. Be honest and thoughtful. Worrying about such questions as "What kind of boss do you prefer?" or "How many hours a day do you think a person should work?" will only pull you away from your game plan of eliciting employer needs and aligning your strengths to those needs.

Cardinal Rules of Interviewing

The Do's

- Smile and show enthusiasm.
- Concentrate on what you can do for your prospective employer, not what they can do for you.
- Show value whenever possible. Appear sought-after.
- Ask questions that show concern for the prospective company and how you can help. Planted seeds may bloom into future meetings or conversations.
- If you have to place any blame or negatives, do it on something impersonal or large, such as the downfall of a particular industry or foreign competition.

The Don'ts

- Don't beat a dead horse. When you've answered a question and have made your point, close your mouth. Try to sense when the interviewer has gotten the message.
- Don't bad-mouth anybody. Even if you know your old boss's reputation is one shade worse than Attila the Hun's, show impartiality and even a capacity to get the best out of any situation. It will give the interviewer the sense that even with Attila as a boss you've been able to keep your spirits up and function in the best way possible.
- Don't ever interrupt or argue with the interviewer. You may win the argument at the interview, but that's all you'll win.
- Don't tell hard-luck stories or beg for the job. No one will hire you out of benevolence.
- Don't mention salary or benefits at the first interview. Your goal is to get the company in a position of really *wanting* you. Then you'll talk compensation.
- Don't ever assume you're winning or losing the interview by the way the interviewer reacts. Stick to your game plan.

The Positive Closing

When you sense the interview is winding down, close with a positive question to wrap it up, but also one that keeps the process moving for you, such as: "Is there any further information I could be reading regarding your company or your products/services?" Or "Is there anything else I can do to show my capabilities?" Or "I'd be glad to tackle any projects on a volunteer basis both to help out and to show you what I can do." Or "What might the next step be?"

The Follow-up

Immediately after the interview you send a short thank-you letter that shows your enthusiasm, touches on the highlights of the interview, and most importantly, keeps the process rolling. "Bob, I've enclosed a recent clipping from *WidgetWorld* that I think complements the marketing ideas we discussed. What do you think? I'll touch base soon with the proposal data I mentioned."

Winning Move #41:

Accumulate Rejection—
Stare in Its Face and
Stick Out Your Tongue

Babe Ruth struck out 1,330 times in his career.

—Anonymous

To win you need to get to the end of the game. And to survive in the face of an inevitable amount of rejection you need a very simple outlook: to want to accumulate rejection as fast as you can. Instead of fearing rejection, you need to look it in the eye and invite it. That's right: *invite rejection*. You will find you'll get used to it. You won't fear it, for you will understand that the job search is a process of accumulating a series of "no's" until you get to a "yes."

The more "no's" that are accumulated, the closer you will get to a "yes." The "no's" are inevitable for all of us; the "no's" are out there, waiting, stacked on top of the winning "yes." There are too many variables involved in the job-match process to expect otherwise. The company needs to like you. You need to like the company. The company needs to have the right culture and philosophy to match yours. The company's product or service needs to appeal to your beliefs. The right position needs to open at the right time. Internal politics have to be in your favor. External economic forces have to be in your favor. In short, there are numerous reasons— *most of them not to be taken personally*—that affect your search.

These reasons are the inevitable curves, sliders, fastballs, and sinkers of the job-search game. You need to accept them as being there and deal with them as they come by you. You must get up to the plate; hiding in the dugout will only prolong your agony.

It is true, Babe Ruth did strike out 1,330 times. That means he swung 3,990 times and missed. But he had to in order to get what he ended up with: 714 home runs!

IV

Shining Examples: Winning Moves From Street-Savvy Job Seekers

A Shining Example of How to Find Hot Companies

To Jonathan Waite, it seemed that every job opening he responded to, he responded to too late! "Sorry, that position has already been filled" was the most common response he got when following up after sending his résumé. He knew it is the early job seeker who catches the job, but how could he get there any earlier? He had to get there *before* his potential employers took action to fill new positions. He knew there must be a solution, but what?

It was when he was reading the Living Section of the *Boston Globe* that his best idea in years hit him. He found several human interest profiles of individuals with hot ideas for a variety of businesses. These seemed to be mostly people with start-up businesses or new divisions who could use someone with talents like his to develop systems and manage growth. The more he thought about it, the more this seemed the right avenue for him to take. There were other sources, such as the Living Section of other newspapers, and magazines that profiled up-and-coming entrepreneurs.

In the business sections of newspapers Jonathan also found stories about new senior-management appointments. Another idea hit him. Here, he thought, might be a good opportunity to approach an executive who, by the nature of his new authority, may be about to do some "housecleaning," bringing in new staff to replace individuals whom he feels are incompetent.

Next Jonathan wrote a letter to each person whose profile or situation intrigued him. The letter complimented the individual on his or her business, then highlighted Jonathan's capabilities to help "reduce the burden of managing all the administrative problems that can come with a growing concern." Then he followed up with a telephone call. He found that the individuals he targeted were often "regular folks" and, once he assured them that he wanted to help them, not sell them something, they were all ears.

The whole process gave Jonathan the inside track, putting him face-to-face with opportunities long before they became available to his fellow job seekers.

Winning Move #43:
A Shining Example of How to Spot Hiring Trends

Ed Roscoe is a Boston-area headhunter whose vocational specialty changes as frequently as the New England weather. Ed makes these changes for good reason. Being in the business of placing people into jobs, it only makes sense for him to work the markets that produce the most jobs. Ed always has plenty of candidates—what he always needs are positions. So he keeps a pulse on the job market to see what's hot and what's not. He does this in three different ways, and you, as a job seeker, can do the same thing.

First, every week Ed counts, by job category, the help-wanted ads in his major area newspapers. He keeps track of the percentage of ads for nurses, programmers, accountants, purchasing agents, and whatever other areas he thinks might be a good specialty. If he notices a dramatic increase in the number of ads in one vocational area, he becomes a headhunter for that area. When the climate changes, he changes.

Second, Ed watches the enrollments at area colleges. If a computer class in Local Area Networking fills up with 52 students in one week, he knows something is hot. If a specialized class doesn't fill or is dropped from the curriculum, he knows something is awry. Ed knows that where there are people paying for specialized training, there are also jobs.

Third, Ed reads well-reputed business and economic trend publications, both local and regional. For example, if he learns in the *Boston Business Journal* that the psychiatric center of a major area hospital has received a large research grant, he'll get in touch with the institution and learn what new staffing needs they're likely to have.

As a job seeker, you can do the same thing that Ed does. Headhunters like Ed may or may not be able to help you find a job, but they're in the same business that you're in: finding and filling positions. And they're pros. Learn from them!

A Shining Example of How to Put Yourself in the Right Place at the Right Time with the Right Person

Helen Fogle knew what she wanted in a career. Her ultimate goal was to become a Director of Human Resources for a major organization. Now that she'd graduated from college, her immediate goal was to obtain a full-time human resources staff position with a good company. But how to break in? She'd developed an excellent broadcast letter and résumé. She'd targeted companies she wanted to get into, then followed up her mailings with a telephone call. But getting through was a different story. It seemed impossible to get the ear of an overworked human resources director besieged with telephone calls from all sorts of human resources vendors, headhunters, and job applicants. If Helen could only get face-to-face with one.

Then she learned about a regional association for human resources professionals. She called them and obtained their literature. She was surprised to learn that the association provided a list of all human resources directors in the Northeast (her area), held specialized human resources training courses and seminars, hosted networking breakfasts and dinners, and even sponsored a human resources placement service. For a reasonable fee Helen was able to join.

She attended the association's first networking event, a dinner held in an area hotel. All the attendees wore name tags listing their title and employer. In the foyer outside the dining room, Helen spotted two of the human resources managers she'd tried to reach on the telephone during her job search. Just as she approached them, the group began moving into the dining room, headed for seats at each of a dozen or so round tables. Helen followed the two managers to their table and sat down right next to them. She was not shy; an hour and a half later they were all friends. Helen had impressed them with her demeanor, her commitment to the field, and her thoughtful questions. Further, and best of all, she'd succeeded in setting up meetings with both managers at their offices the following week. And she did all this before dessert was served! Not bad for a rookie job seeker.

A Shining Example of How to Network with Well-Connected Groups of People Who Know Your Value

Steve Sipplin was a capable radio industry professional who lost his job in the very difficult Boston area job market of 1991. In nine months, Steve still didn't have any solid job prospects on the horizon. He knew he was multi-talented and well respected in the community, and he knew that radio wasn't all he could do. He wasn't about to sell his house in a depressed real estate market. And he didn't want to uproot his family to relocate. He was running out of options. He kept hearing the term "networking" from friends and fellow job seekers. And then it occurred to him: The group of people who knew him well and were the best-connected professionals were the parents at his children's private school. He decided to tap into them via a targeted form letter. Here's what it said:

Dear Fellow Holten School Parent:

First, please excuse the form letter. Obviously, though, it's pretty much the only way to handle the situation. Lori and I, like countless victims of our devastated Massachusetts economy, are at a crossroads. Unless a job opportunity arises soon, we'll be forced to move to another part of the country to accept one of two job offers I've received. We're certainly not asking for any sympathy, only some networking on the part of our friends and fellow Holten parents to possibly precipitate an opportunity.

The product you would be networking for is solid. My résumé is included here. What else can I add? I've succeeded in virtually all areas of my profession. I've owned and operated a national broadcast production company. I've been president of a Fortune 500 company division. I'm a highly capable manager and proven team-builder, and skilled in press/public relations, marketing, and events production.

While this may seem a bit of an unorthodox approach to job seeking, I guess it reflects part of my style. And, frankly, over the last twenty years, some of my best moves and strategies have been just that: unorthodox. And usually successful!

I'm open to bringing my talents and experience to any number of industries. If you know of any opportunities for which I may be suited, please give me a call at 953-1556. I hope to continue being a Holten parent!

Sincerely,

Steve's letter brought him several surprises, including a phone call from a senior vice president of a major public relations firm in Boston who liked Steve's style *and* liked his national experience promoting live-via-satellite events.

They talked. And they talked again. And then they struck a deal that allowed Steve to continue being a Holten parent!

A Shining Example of How to Create Networking Relationships with Total Strangers

Cathy Lester, a paralegal from Boston, used the following networking approach to get the inside track in a very specific area of interest.

In her job as a paralegal, she had assisted in several cases involving Workers Compensation fraud. The fraud abuse in the system both interested her and annoyed her. There was obviously a problem, so she figured there must be an emerging job market for providing solutions.

Cathy felt her skills, interests, and attitudes would be an asset to those concerned with remedying the situation. But where to look? All she could seem to find was general information from the insurance industry or write-ups of specialized legal cases. Then she went to the *Encyclopedia of Associations* and found the name of a major Workers Compensation association. Figuring they would have knowledge of where she should look next, she called them and learned that there were a growing number of small, emerging organizations in business to consult with companies on avoiding or investigating Workers Compensation fraud. The association didn't know of any small firms in her area—these new companies weren't well organized yet as a group, they said—but she might look for their advertisements in the national insurance industry trade magazines. They yielded the names of a couple.

While looking for advertisements for this kind of service, Cathy stumbled upon several articles on Workers Compensation fraud. The articles gave her more information and knowledge. One in particular made reference to the Boston area. She called the magazine and obtained the author's address. In her letter to him she flattered the author on his insight into the issues, noted some of his more salient points, and asked if she might call him for more information about career opportunities in that field.

A week later the author called her. They met in Boston for lunch, and within an hour's time Cathy had a notepad full of specialized information regarding key individuals and companies in the Boston area who served her area of interest. Further, by the end of lunch the author was beginning to act in a mentoring role, indicating he would take Cathy under his wing and provide some introductions that would get her in the door. Cathy was off and running!

Winning Move #47:
A Shining Example of an Irresistible Cover Letter

Paula Mishkin, a Sales Support Specialist, developed a cover letter that generated an excellent response because she kept her reader's needs in mind. She asked herself, "Knowing what I know about my field, if I was hiring a Sales Support Specialist, what would I look for?" Then she developed a letter (see page 168) that answered the question.

John Alston
Vice President of Sales
Farnsworth Industrial
Stoughton Industrial Park
Stoughton, MA 02253

RE: *Sales Support Specialist* position

Dear Mr. Alston:

As a highly skilled *Sales Support Specialist* having successful experience with such companies as PictureTel, Webster Industries, and L.L. Bean, I am responding to your recent advertisement for a Sales Support Specialist.

As you can see from the enclosed, I am a team worker with more than nine years of direct experience understanding and servicing the needs of field sales. Further, I am computer literate, can effectively manage multiple priorities, have a foundation in materials management, and have degrees in marketing and management.

Finally, I am driven to provide the Total Quality and Service approach to customers.

My salary requirement is in the thirties.

Should Farnsworth Industrial be able to benefit from my background, abilities, and expertise in Sales Support, I would be pleased to meet with you to discuss the opportunity.

Sincerely yours,

Paula Mishkin

enclosure: résumé

Notice that Paula mentions the opening to which she's responding *before* the body of the letter. This clearly identifies the purpose of the letter without taking up valuable space in her lead. She knows the lead to her letter (the first sentence) must grab Mr. Alston's attention with some of the most valuable points of her background. She doesn't want to weaken her lead with an impotent sentence such as "Enclosed please find my résumé in response to..." or "I am seeking an opportunity as a Sales Support Specialist..." These leads don't convey any information about Paula. So Paula begins her cover letters with the words "As a." This forces her to describe herself and makes writing the letter easier, allowing self-descriptive words to flow. But best of all, it qualifies her, giving Mr. Alston the valuable information that she's already worked in Sales Support at major companies.

In the next paragraph Paula uses more ammunition, informing Mr. Alston of her most relevant professional skills. This is the paragraph she alters to the needs of each position she sees advertised, picking her skills that most closely match the requirements of the job. For example, Paula knows that "Total Quality and Service" is an important industry buzz phrase, so she uses it in her letter.

This position advertisement also asked for salary requirements. Paula is clever here by saying "in the thirties." That could be $30,000 or $39,000. It doesn't lock her in too high or too low.

In her closing paragraph, Paula adds a self-assured tone, keeping in mind the needs of her reader. She uses the powerful words "benefit" and "opportunity" in connection with her own value. In her last sentence, Paula doesn't say that she will be calling to follow up or that she will wait to hear from Mr. Alston. Even though she definitely plans to follow up in several days, she leaves her closing open-ended so as not to appear too aggressive, and also to allow Mr. Alston the chance to call her if he wishes.

Paula's letter is intentionally short. It has been her experience that long cover letters just don't get read. She's learned that a short, "punchy" letter, like good advertising copy, gets the busy reader's attention.

Paula knows how to sell herself on paper. Perhaps her next step from Sales Support should be into Sales!

A Shining Example of a Telephone Technique That Will Help You Sell Yourself

Bill Homan had had a long job search. He dreaded the thought of any more rejection. Even worse, it was getting to the point that he almost asked for it, because he knew he came across like a well-used punching bag just asking for more.

Then a friend in sales told him of an old telemarketing trick. "It's been done ever since there have been telephones," Bill's friend said. "If you look at yourself in a mirror and smile while speaking on the phone, the tone of your voice will improve, your voice will become more animated, and your overall attitude will improve. Try it! It will make follow-ups easier and much more productive."

And that's what Bill Homan did. He found that it had taken much more energy to frown and otherwise look dejected. It used more muscles. So he began smiling. He smiled into the mirror while on the telephone. He smiled while networking. He smiled during his research at the library. He smiled at interviews.

And he smiled when the right prospective employer said, "Yes!"

Winning Move #49:

A Shining Example of How to Impress Your Interviewer

For several years Bill Southberry had wanted to leave his position as a commercial real estate broker and get into management consulting. His background also included analytical work in the medical field and an M.B.A., which he'd earned over the past several years. Finally, his big break came. The principal of a leading ophthalmology practice management consulting firm needed to add a staff consultant and had agreed to interview Bill. The ideal person needed an M.B.A., account development (sales) skills, strong analytical abilities, and medical experience (ideally in an ophthalmic office environment). Bill had all but the latter. He felt well equipped to go into the interview and promote his account development, business, and analytical skills. But his medical exposure was not in ophthalmology. Bill knew he'd have the edge if only he had some exposure to the workings of an ophthalmology practice.

It was his wife who came up with the solution. "Why not call that ophthalmologist who treated your eye injury several years ago?" she asked. "You said you two got along real well and even talked about going sailing together. Why not tell him your situation and see if he might show you around his practice and answer some of your questions?"

And that was just what Bill did. In fact, Dr. Norman, the ophthalmologist whom Bill visited, knew of the management consulting firm for which Bill would be interviewing. He was more than glad to show Bill the workings of his practice and outline the kind of practice management problems he typically faced. Bill took notes and asked plenty of questions. And he promised to take Dr. Norman sailing!

In his interview the following week Bill felt much more comfortable than he had anticipated. When his interviewer asked him why he felt he could handle the job, Bill said, "My blend of medical experience, my M.B.A., my proven sales ability, and my familiarity with the workings of an ophthalmology practice." He went on to explain that, first, during his own eye treatments he took interest in the busy, sometimes disorganized and chaotic business operations of the ophthalmic practice. Later he did some research on his own, asking an ophthalmologist about the typical and specialized nature of business operational problems within the practice. This impressed Bill's interviewer. Not only did Bill show "product" knowledge, but he showed that he was the kind of person who prepared for an interview, did his research, and thoughtfully presented his findings.

Bill found himself a good job!

Winning Move #50:

A Shining Example of How to Win the Job *After* You're Turned Down

Mary Ellen Hild didn't win the job at first. But she interviewed well and the company liked her. After she received what she could only term a very positive rejection letter, she filed it away and went about her job search.

Then something occurred to her. "Hey, wait a minute," she said to herself. Coming in second counts for a lot. They said they had more than 100 applicants. They said they interviewed five. That puts me in the top 2 percentile. And they liked me. I've already been inside the organization. They've spent time and money getting to know me. I shouldn't just walk away!"

So Mary Ellen wrote a thank-you letter to her interviewer after she received her rejection letter. It looked like this:

Dear George:

Needless to say, it was a sad day when I received your letter of 6/12 and learned of my dubious distinction of being your second choice. I felt so comfortable meeting all of you and discussing the goals of Emmel Corporation.

Despite the fact that there's not a spot for me at the moment, you folks are still my first choice, as I feel we complement each other and that my skills would dovetail nicely with the needs of Emmel.

I won't let you off the hook that easily! Please allow me to keep in touch and stay informed of new developments at Emmel. And if there's any special project I could help you with in the meantime, don't hesitate to call.

Regardless of my own personal outcome with Emmel, I wish you all the most prosperous future and best of luck with your new employee.

Kind regards,

Mary Ellen had come too far to burn any bridges, and she felt that it would be only a matter of time until the company called her. Because they'd already interviewed her and knew her talents, she would be a quick and easy addition to the staff. And she knew that the company was growing. Besides, for any number of reasons, their first-choice employee might not work out.

Six weeks later she found out that she was right!

Epigraph

This is where I get off and you keep going. And go you will. You'll keep going because you know you have value. You'll keep going because you know you are marketable. And you'll keep going because you have the tools to get you where you want to go.

Odds are you'll get there.

I'm betting on it.